ORGANIZING FOOD, FAITH AND FREEDOM

Organizations and Activism

Series Editors: **Daniel King**, Nottingham Trent University and **Martin Parker**, University of Bristol

From co-operatives to corporations, Occupy to Facebook, organizations shape our lives. They engage in politics as well as shaping the possible futures of policy making and social change. This series publishes books that explore how politics happens within and because of organizations, how activism is organized, and how activists change organizations.

Scan the code below to discover new and forthcoming titles in the series, or visit:

bristoluniversitypress.co.uk/
organizations-and-activism

ORGANIZING FOOD, FAITH AND FREEDOM

Imagining Alternatives

Ozan Nadir Alakavuklar

BRISTOL
UNIVERSITY
PRESS

First published in Great Britain in 2024 by

Bristol University Press
University of Bristol
1–9 Old Park Hill
Bristol
BS2 8BB
UK
t: +44 (0)117 374 6645
e: bup-info@bristol.ac.uk

Details of international sales and distribution partners are available at bristoluniversitypress.co.uk

British Library Cataloguing in Publication Data
A catalogue record for this book is available from the British Library

ISBN 978-1-5292-1623-3 hardcover
ISBN 978-1-5292-1625-7 ePub
ISBN 978-1-5292-1626-4 ePdf

Cover design: blu inc
Front cover image: CanStock Photo/zenstock
Bristol University Press use environmentally responsible print partners.
Printed and bound in Great Britain by CPI Group (UK) Ltd, Croydon, CR0 4YY

FSC
www.fsc.org
MIX
Paper | Supporting
responsible forestry
FSC® C013604

To Doruk,

with the hope of a socially just and
ecologically sustainable world full of
alternatives he cherishes

Contents

Series Editors' Preface

Daniel King and Martin Parker

Organizing is politics made durable. From cooperatives to corporations, Occupy to Meta, states to NGOs, organizations shape our lives. They shape the possible futures of governance, policy making and social change, and hence are central to understanding how we can deal with the challenges that face us, whether that be pandemics, populism or climate change. This book series publishes work that explores how politics happens within and because of organizations and organizing. We want to explore how activism is organized and how activists change organizations. We are also interested in the forms of resistance to activism, the ways that powerful interests contest and reframe demands for change. These are questions of huge relevance to scholars in sociology, politics, geography, management and beyond, and are becoming ever more important as demands for impact and engagement change the way that academics imagine their work. They are also important to anyone who wants to understand more about the theory and practice of organizing, not just the abstracted ideologies of capitalism taught in business schools.

Our books offer critical examinations of organizations as sites of or targets for activism, and we also assume that our authors, and hopefully our readers, are themselves agents of change. Titles may focus on specific industries or fields, or they may be arranged around particular themes or challenges. Our topics might include the alternative economy; surveillance, whistleblowing and human rights; digital politics; religious groups; social movements; NGOs; feminism and anarchist organization; action research and coproduction; activism and the neoliberal university – or any other subjects that are relevant and topical.

Organizations and Activism is also a multidisciplinary series. Contributions from all and any relevant academic fields will be welcomed. The series is international in outlook, and proposals from outside the English-speaking Global North are particularly welcome.

This book, the seventh in our series, examines some of the most vital aspects of our lives – food, faith and freedom. In this personal and informative account, Ozan Alakavuklar invites you into the world of the Free Food Store and the experiences he had participating as a volunteer there. *Organizing Food, Faith and Freedom* provides a detailed and lovingly written account of the everyday practices involved within the Free Food Store, and in so doing draws out the wider social, political and organizational implications of the work it does.

Central to this book is food. More specifically, how organizations like the Free Food Store challenge an essential contraction which lies at the heart of capitalism. On the one hand we have food waste. Millions of tonnes of perfectly edible food is either dumped in landfill or, as Alakavuklar describes, becomes a feast for pigs. This is a clear sign of the profligacy of the capitalist system, not only costing money but also causing unnecessary rises in carbon emissions and doing significant harm to the planet. On the other hand we have people going hungry, unable to afford some of the basic essentials to survive. This, as Alakavuklar stresses, is seriously wrong – and it is what the Free Food Store tries to fix.

The store does this by taking food that would otherwise go to waste and giving it away for free. Their joint mission is to ensure that no one faces hunger and to minimize food wastage. While, on the surface, this might seem like a food bank, the Free Food Store is different. Customers are not means-tested as they are in food banks; there is no need to prove poverty through a voucher or referral. The Free Food Store is open to anyone. Importantly, they not only provide nonperishable food – tins, packets, and so on, donated by people trying to help out – but also offer perishable food that would otherwise become waste. Therefore, they are about connecting surplus food, which they call 'rescued food', with people who need it, to challenge the normal economic model of food production and consumption. The Free Food Store can be considered a form of social and solidarity economy organized around the community's needs.

This book is more than just an ethnography of the Free Food Store; it is an activist tale. Ozan is highly engaged in the shop, getting his hands literally dirty by sorting potatoes and other perishable food items. This opens a divide and an unending set of questions and tensions between his activist self and academic self as he wrestles to navigate between these two ways of being. Bringing this tension to the foreground, *Organizing Food, Faith and Freedom* is also an attempt at writing differently, a dialogue between the activist self and the academic self.

We hope you enjoy this book. And if you want to discuss your own proposal, then email the series editors. We look forward to hearing from you.

List of Figures and Tables

Figures

Tables

Acknowledgements

Like many other published monographs, this book has been a product of many years of dedication and collaboration. Since my fieldwork at the Free Food Store, which took place between January and September 2015, I have devoted myself to reading, thinking, talking and writing about alternatives and organizing. Many colleagues and friends have witnessed and contributed to the development of my ideas, providing invaluable input. I extend my heartfelt thanks to Craig Prichard, Andrew Dickson, Fahreen Alamgir, Suze Wilson, Ralph Bathurst, Damian Ruth, Patrizia Zanoni, Raza Mir, Nicholas Roelants and Aykut Dağkıran for their collegiality, support, guidance and wisdom. I also would like to thank my colleagues at Utrecht University School of Governance for their feedback on various chapters of the book. As Organizations and Activism series co-editors, Daniel King and Martin Parker provided very helpful guidance when I was developing my ideas in the early stages of preparing the book – sincere thanks to them for their support.

I am profoundly grateful to the Free Food Store's founder/director, manager and volunteers for welcoming me and endorsing my research. Their support has given me the opportunity to explore who I want to be and what I want to achieve as a scholar.

I also want to express my gratitude to Paul Stevens from Bristol University Press, who initially approached me and encouraged me to turn my dream of writing a book into a reality. His colleagues, Ellen Pearce, Isobel Green and Rich Kemp, have played a crucial editorial role in bringing this book to life. Furthermore, I would like to thank production editor Sophia Unger from Newgen for her support and meticulous work.

I extend my sincere thanks to my parents, Mehmet and Esen, and my brother, Onur, for their unwavering encouragement and belief in me. Finally, I want to offer my deepest appreciation to my wife, Deniz – none of this would have been possible without your love and support.

Copyright notice

Chapters 2, 4 and 6 are revised versions of the previously published work:

Introduction

Dear reader (if you do not mind my addressing you this way) ...

I know how unusual it is to begin a scholarly book like this. Nevertheless, throughout the book, rather than offering a cold, detached, technical account of my research, I aim to converse with you, taking you through my (academic) journey. Not only will you read about an interesting organizational case, but you will encounter the transformation story of an early career academic. As I open up my 'self' throughout the book, I make the assumption that you are with me in this journey as a reader but, more importantly, as a companion.

When I address you, I imagine you are among a group of readers comprised of students, academics, activists, policy makers and professionals who are broadly interested in alternative, community-based, bottom-up organizing around food within and beyond neoliberal capitalist relations. This comes with the challenge of finding a common narrative thread that can potentially cut across all readers' interests, but that aside, I hope you, my dear reader, will find it valuable to be confronted with the theoretically informed idea of 'writing differently' (Gilmore et al, 2019; Boncori, 2022). The theory, in an accessible 'reading', will be with us throughout the journey.

The overall argument of this book is based on demonstrating the complex layers of organizing at the margins and thinking about and imagining emancipatory alternative organizing forms in a world which is becoming increasingly grim given the impact of climate catastrophe, (post-)pandemic conditions and rising socioeconomic inequality. Nevertheless, by focusing on my choices and providing retrospective reflection, this book tells the story of an academic finding his way in the (neoliberal) academy across three countries – Turkey, Aotearoa New Zealand and the Netherlands. My engagement with theories and methods cannot be considered independent of my context – my moving between countries and noting similarities and differences, and the global undercurrent of neoliberal values promoting individualized performance measurements, rankings and competition in higher education institutions.

Let me begin by setting out the background to my introduction to the notion of alternatives – not only alternative organizations but also an alternative critical and academic activist modality. If I count my undergraduate degree, I spent more than 12 years at a business school in Turkey – which kept me busy, as a student, learning, and as a research assistant, studying 'management and organization' broadly. Hence, I have been on both sides of 'business and management education' for quite a long time. I came to know the specific field of critical management and organization studies in the second year of my PhD, and that changed everything. Given this field's general assumptions and critique about the orthodoxy in management studies, I knew it was one I wanted to be part of, though at the time I didn't know much about its history, tensions and challenges (Alakavuklar, 2017). Despite its contested position within business schools, it opened a new and transformative path for me to discover more about the broader critical tradition within the social sciences, which has informed my teaching, research and activism.

My first academic post was as a lecturer in Aotearoa New Zealand. This was where the fieldwork, the subject of this book, took place and where I had the freedom to express my ethical and political choices in an academic context and realized what I want to do as an academic (see more on this in Chapter 6). It was quite a journey, with wonderful colleagues, from whom I learned a lot, exchanged ideas and developed research projects. Since July 2019, I have been working in the Netherlands at Utrecht University School of Governance, which is, again, a completely different cultural, institutional and social context. Here, I transitioned to mid-career academic level, with a more focused research agenda and more responsibilities in the academic community.

You may wonder about my motivation for relocating, considering the diverse national contexts and challenges I encountered when changing institutions, countries and even continents. While the expectations of my family and (enabling/constraining) institutional regimes influenced my decisions, what I was looking for was a nurturing environment for my critical organization research. I sought critical scholarly communities to support my intellectual growth and foster collaboration for exciting academic projects. That search led me to find a 'home' outside a business school, a place with an explicit focus on 'critical organization studies'.

The experience cutting through these three countries is based on understanding and contesting oppressive and orthodox (organizational) regimes and practices, and thinking about 'alternatives' and alternative organizational forms. Having grown up in a dynamic developing country stuck between the East and the West, with a background of post-coup developments and trying to find its place in a global economy through neoliberal reforms throughout the 1980s and 1990s, I was driven by the motivation to bring change and transformation for social justice. However, it took me many years to find the relevant language and theoretical tools that would help me not only make sense of my own country's context, the role of business schools and dominant capitalist relations imposing particular subjectivities (Alakavuklar and Parker, 2011), but also move forwards to frame and theorize alternatives. This book is a modest attempt at this purpose.

Alternative as a concept, then, refers to thinking, acting, studying and imagining differently about the way we organize our economy and society. If we begin with the problematization of apolitical, acontextual and ahistorical modes of organizing, as in the case of using corporations as *the* model in business schools and assuming capitalist relations as the norm (Boyacigiller and Adler, 1991; Alakavuklar, 2014; Parker, 2018), alternatives can be seen as the entry points for showing the diversity, difference and richness of other forms of organizing for socially just and ecologically sustainable societies.

What makes this book worthy of interest? Depending on your expectations, my dear reader, there might be different factors; but from my end, I want to bring a refreshing perspective to understanding community initiatives as alternative organizations and share what my engagement with them has taught me. Through my fieldwork experience, I primarily learned to reconcile my scholarly preconceptions with the actual dynamics of community organization. This involved discerning whether the intent was geared towards political transformation. I discovered a greater diversity of economic practices than I had initially envisioned. For me, this diversity of multiple practices around food, faith and freedom was indeed the source of alternatives and imaginaries.

Outline of the chapters

In this chapter, before getting into the theoretical openings, I detail the background of, and my motivation for engaging in, the research discussed in this book – the reason I am interested in alternative organizations, my assumptions about social science and organization studies, and how I ended up doing fieldwork at the Free Food Store, a pioneering food rescue organization that provides free food to the community.

In Chapter 2, I share my initial questions about the Free Food Store, based on my observations there, to identify the layers of complexity in this small charity shop. It is like a sample of the following chapters, demonstrating the richness of my case and my struggle to position my self with ethical and political commitments in the field.

In Chapter 3, I delve into the role of faith and religion as the cultural/ symbolic layer in the organizing of the Free Food Store and its relative surrender to neoliberal logic against the background of increasing poverty and inequality in Aotearoa New Zealand. I discuss the potential for mobilizing communities by faith to address social issues, and I demonstrate how the potential transformative edge of faith is neutralized by neoliberal policies, leading inevitably to limited politicization of food poverty while there is, at the same time, problematization of food surplus. I argue how a political-economic project (that is, neoliberalism) subsumes moral cause, while the morality of the faith still has the potential for imagining alternatives within these constraints.

In Chapter 4, my focus shifts from the cultural/symbolic layer to the economic/material layer. Drawing on Marxian literature, I argue how the use value of surplus food and volunteer labour mediates noncapitalist organizational relations amid capitalist practices. This is a novel perspective for discussing, first, the relationship between use value and exchange value in an economy where diverse capitalist and noncapitalist practices are entangled and, second, how the Free Food Store serves as a case for demonstrating the complexity of this entanglement. It attempts to decentre 'capital-o-centrism' and centre the potentiality of diverse economic practices to theorize alternative organizing within and beyond capitalist relations.

In Chapter 5, I share my insights regarding the role of power relations within the Free Food Store. I claim that a particular 'mediation' of an ensemble of discourses and practices (that is, the Foucauldian 'dispositive') creates 'disciplined freedom' for the shop's customers. I argue that freedom in a 'free shop' has its own limitations and governing practices. Concerning analysis of the symbolic, economic and political layers of the Free Food Store, mediation is a critical concept. It is a term I borrow from Marxian analysis to explain how constructs such as faith, the use value of things and a particular form of politics shape social and organizational relations – in other words, how they bind actors and their meso-level practices with macro-level structures.

In Chapter 6, I introduce 'activist performativity', a term based on the lessons I learned at the Free Food Store, and offer an alternative organizational scholarship that attempts to align research, teaching and activism holistically within the defined boundary conditions I found myself in. I also detail my attempts to become an 'academic activist' and call for more engagement with grassroots and community organizations.

Finally, in Chapter 7, I connect the dots and build an overarching conclusion based on the preceding chapters, through the notion of 'weak theorizing'. I advance the discussion concerning the role of community organizations and their limitations and potential in my search for alternatives, and I emphasize the importance of (co-)imagining combined with academic activism, which the university can facilitate as an anchor institution and partner for social change.

While each chapter has its own theoretical orientation and specific contributions to scholarly conversations, as you will note, I benefit from diverse intellectual strands and disciplines and draw arguments from sociology, human geography, anthropology and organization studies. While you can certainly enjoy reading the chapters individually, the sequence in which they are presented offers a more coherent and insightful perspective on the journey I intend to take you on. As I do my best to address you, my dear reader, I am aware that Chapters 4, 5 and 7 may still lean in to the theory side, yet they are still written with the purpose of making theory accessible. I hope you bear with me in this personal, organizational and theoretical journey till the end.

The study of food

At this point, I'd like to open a parenthesis and address the topic of 'food' in my study, given its central role in my organizational case. Food is a subject of study in various fields, having been explored by anthropologists (Klein and Watson, 2016), sociologists (Murcott, 2019), geographers (Kneafsey et al, 2021), economists (Clapp, 2016), philosophers (Kaplan, 2019) and historians (Pilcher, 2012), among others. Hence, food is a rich and multidimensional concept, encompassing material, symbolic, sensual and multifaceted aspects that cut across various disciplines (Murcott, 2013; Gustafsson et al, 2019). That is why 'food studies' (Miller and Deutsch, 2009; Albala, 2013; Koç et al, 2016) emerges as an interdisciplinary field that fosters cross-disciplinary scholarly conversations. Moreover, there are multiple avenues through which food can be studied, including: food systems and food regimes, which mainly focus on governance, production, supply and distribution relationships; food waste, from economic, moral and political perspectives; food politics, covering issues like food justice, food sovereignty, food activism and movements, and alternative food networks; and food insecurity and food poverty (Murcott et al, 2013; Atkins and Bowler, 2016; Sage, 2022).

While the focus on food has been relatively marginal in management and organization studies (Briner and Sturdy, 2008), there has been a growing interest, as evidenced by special issues in the journals *Human Relations*, *Organization* and *Organization Studies*.[1] Recognizing the central role of food in our organizational lives, Pina e Cunha et al (2008) posit it is explored indirectly in the studies of management, work and organizations. They argue food offers multiple entry points to 'better understand organizations and the process of organizing by studying the way organizations deal with food' (Pina e Cunha et al, 2008, p 936). This includes examining food as a

---

[1] *Human Relations* (2008), 61(7); *Organization* (2020) 27(2); *Organization Studies* (2021), 42(2).

fundamental need, a driver of social interaction, a cultural and institutional element and a source of critique and metaphor (Pina e Cunha et al, 2008, pp 955–956).

Moser et al point out that not only do we organize our lives around food, but food and its biomaterial characteristics organize, shape and structure our lives and practices: 'food, organisations and organising are thus deeply intertwined' (2021, p 176). They propose a two-dimensional framework that considers: food as an object of and context for organizing; and the agentic capability of food and organizations. While the former focuses on how organizing takes place around food for our survival, the latter offers a broader perspective on the role of food as the organizing force that impacts organizational efforts.

Furthermore, Böhm et al (2020) take a structural and critical approach to studying food from an organizational perspective through the 'labour' aspect. They invite critical organization scholars 'to lift the commodity veil and to explore the production and organization processes behind food and the context that shapes them' (Böhm et al, 2020, p 197) and 'to take the human labour element in food more seriously, from farm or sea to consumption and waste' (p 198). They underscore the significance, variety and politics of food labour within the changing landscape of global agrifood systems to address the established and new forms of food labour processes.

As you can see, my dear reader, food is an exciting and relevant topic for organizational research! While it is a (bio)material item to meet the needs of people, it is more than that in the sense of organizing social relations and interactions, and shaping organizational practices around it. Therefore, my study is centred on the 'social organizing of food' (Moser et al, 2021) and incorporates a structural critique (Pina e Cunha et al, 2008; Böhm et al, 2020). In this context, 'surplus food' takes on an agentic role, enabling the Free Food Store through the mediation of faith, labour and power relations. Let me close the parenthesis here and take you back to our journey together.

How my journey began

In 2014, one year after moving to Aotearoa New Zealand, I was striving to find my own way and voice in academia. Having completed a PhD in Business Administration in Turkey, my post at Massey University (Palmerston North) was my first official lectureship. As a self-identified critical management and organization scholar, positioned in the long tradition of critical scholarship in business schools (Adler et al, 2007; Wharerata Writing Group, 2018) and drawing from multiple theories, my overall research goal was to offer theoretical openings about alternative organizations and their transformative potential.

This focus on alternative organizing and its practices did not come out of the blue. Since the critical tradition in business schools has been criticized because of its heavy technical and philosophical jargon, its lack of relevance to societal challenges, its limited impact on managerial and organizational practice, and its inward discussions concerning how the 'critique' should have been done (Dunne et al, 2008; Fleming and Banerjee, 2016), there was a need to respond to the 'so what' question: if the issues centre on hierarchical relations, limited participation in decision making and inequitable resource distribution, what can critical scholars offer in terms of alternative solutions at various levels?

The overarching concern has revolved around the prevailing economic practices contributing to socioeconomic disparities and sustainability challenges, in which academics, activists and practitioners attempt to intervene (Parker et al, 2014b). The big question is how to organize the economy and society so that the organizational practices could lead to democratic decision-making processes, socioeconomic equality and fair distribution of resources. There is not an easy answer to such a big question, given that all these ideals are not only contested but also the results of centuries-long mobilizations and struggles. Within the tradition of critical management and organization studies, beginning with the question of resistance within and beyond organizations (Alakavuklar, 2012; Alakavuklar and Alamgir, 2018), alternative organizing and alternative economies seemed to me the relevant path to take, as they potentially and critically transform norms, identities, practices and communities.

In my new position, and setting, in Aotearoa New Zealand, the challenge was to find an appropriate organization where I could study the idea of alternative-ness concerning the ongoing societal challenges through the principles of participatory, engaged research. The real difficulty was how to translate this inspiration into a structured process that would allow me to make a meaningful contribution to an organization's broader objectives. The notion of 'contribution' to the organization was essential since, politically and ethically, I could not agree with the idea and practice of the 'detached scientist' observing others. Having opposed the positivist epistemological claims of the possibility of a distant and objective researcher, I had already embraced the notion of critical social science that is supposed to unmask power relations and, if possible, contribute to the practice of societal transformation. Nevertheless, these were 'concepts in theory' which I needed to test. I was eager and motivated, but it was unclear how, and through which theoretical, methodological and political processes, I could achieve that. It was my first attempt at organizational ethnography that allowed me to delve into the alternatives and, in a way, go down a 'rabbit hole' of economic and social transformation through organizing differently (Parker et al, 2014b; Schiller-Merkens, 2022).

The context of Aotearoa New Zealand

As a member country of the Organisation for Economic Co-operation and Development, Aotearoa New Zealand is considered a 'developed' country. It had a gross domestic product per capita of US$48,249 in 2022 (World Bank, nd), and is ranked 13 (out of 191 countries and territories) on the Human Development Index in 2021 (United Nations Development Programme, nd). Despite the perception of the country as an exotic heaven, with nature and isolation that has attracted billionaires (Clarke, 2022), it has various socioeconomic challenges that have emerged due to its economic transformation in the 1980s, referred to as the neoliberal experiment (Kelsey, 1995). As of 2023, Aotearoa New Zealand faces issues of growing unemployment, rising cost of living, institutional racism and food poverty in addition to the pressures of (post-)pandemic conditions.

It seems a striking contradiction that people have food access issues in a country which officially promotes itself as

a world leader in food production and one of the world's top food exporters, providing millions of people in over 120 countries with premium food and beverage products. New Zealand exports more dairy products, lamb and venison than any other country, and is among the leading exporters of beef, kiwifruit, apples and seafood. (Invest New Zealand, 2023)

While food is abundant in this country, as elsewhere, there are significant issues regarding food poverty and access to healthy food. While this has been exacerbated by the COVID-19 pandemic, there were already significant issues before that. For instance, in 2017, families asking for food parcels from The Salvation Army food banks increased by 12 per cent compared to the previous year (Johnson, 2018). The number of one-off food grants and their cost to the government rose significantly in 2018, with a 50 per cent rise from 2016 (Bracewell-Worrall, 2018). Moreover, according to the *Child Poverty Monitor* report, in 2016 approximately 135,000 New Zealand children (12 per cent) experienced a forced lack of seven or more essential items, including fresh fruit, vegetables and meat (Duncanson et al, 2017, p 3).

(Post-)pandemic conditions in Aotearoa New Zealand have made the affordability and accessibility of food more difficult. The Salvation Army delivered 113,000 food parcels nationally by the end of 2020, almost double compared with 2019 (Tanielu, 2021). According to Growing Up in New Zealand (2023), based on data collected in 2021–2022, 15 per cent of 12-year-olds lived in moderately food insecure households and 2 per cent lived in households with severe food insecurity. Difficulties relating to rising living costs and inflationary pressures are also reported in the New Zealand

Food Network's 2023 annual report, which states that their food hubs were feeding 165 per cent more compared to the beginning of 2020, before the pandemic (New Zealand Food Network, 2023a). The same survey shows a 20 per cent increase in demand for food support in the six months to June 2023 compared to the six months to December 2022 (New Zealand Food Network, 2023b). Meanwhile, food waste in retail is estimated at 13 kilograms per capita per year (Goodman-Smith et al, 2020) and, according to a research conducted in 2017/2018, 24,372 tonnes metric of food is thrown away annually by cafes and restaurants in Aotearoa New Zealand (Mainvil et al, 2018).

Overall, there is a morally and politically unacceptable and striking gap when it comes to the amount of food waste and those who do not have adequate access to food. This is also an indication of a structural problem of income inequality and (re)distribution of wealth, which has led to, for instance, the Māori and Pacifica communities living disproportionately below the poverty line and higher risks of child poverty in the case of Aotearoa New Zealand (Rashbrooke, 2013, pp 4–5). The city I lived in, a small town with a population of around 90,000 and located between the centre and south end of the North Island, was not free of these problems.

As I settled in after my move from Turkey, I had not yet become aware of the scale of these socioeconomic challenges. Thanks to my colleague Craig Prichard, I learned of the Free Food Store – a food rescue organization registered as a charity shop, which problematizes food waste, collects surplus food from different retailers and redistributes it without any monetary transaction. This was a surprising coincidence, since I had already noted the large queues that formed in front of a shop at a petrol station in the heart of the city. Why would people queue at a petrol station shop? It turned out that this was the Free Food Store. I sensed that this would be an important topic to think and write about. After email communication with Mary,[2] the Free Food Store's director (who was also the founder), in which I informed her about my motivation to explore the work of the shop, she agreed that I could access the shop to do volunteer work. My plan was to immerse myself, through participant observation, in the organizational activities and get to know the organizational actors, day-to-day practices and relations.

At this point, I need to emphasize that getting university ethics approval for this research took some time. Here, I encountered for the first time the challenges of convincing an ethics committee on my approach to methodological, ethical and political choices I would have to make in the field. I was aware of the criticisms concerning the institutionalization of ethics in universities and the limitations for social scientists (Schrag, 2011).

---

[2] Mary is a pseudonym used to protect the confidentiality of the founder/director.

I had to negotiate on the clarity of my title for the research project and the details of the information sheet. Of course, these steps are carried out with good intention, and they indeed sensitize researchers to potential ethical (and political) conflicts. Nevertheless, as claimed by Clegg et al (2007), ethics is not something that can be managed; it emerges in the process, in the moments when dilemmas are encountered. Luckily, I did not have to deal with any serious ethical dilemmas during my research.

Engaging with the Free Food Store

Against the backdrop of (food) poverty amid abundance, the shop operates at the heart of the North Island of Aotearoa New Zealand. It was founded in 2011 by Mary, a churchgoer who used to redistribute surplus food (mostly loaves of bread) by her individual efforts (independent of an organized shop). She believed the situation with excess food becoming waste was morally and environmentally unacceptable. As a solution, she collaborated locally – with academics, businesses and the local council – in order to redistribute a greater volume of food through a shop.

The shop's joint mission is not to let anyone go hungry and to reduce food waste. They collect donated fresh perishable food as well as nonperishable food and let customers have it in a shop setting without any monetary exchange. The surplus food comes from around 60 suppliers, including big retailers, local cafes and individuals. Mary and the shop manager, John,[3] work part-time and are supported by volunteers.

My fieldwork was designed as an ethnographic case study at the organizational level (Thomas, 2015) to engage deeply with the organizational practices, meanings and context of the Free Food Store. As a participant observer, I volunteered in the shop for eight months to be part of the daily routines and practices organized around food surplus (hence, the reference to organizing food). Sometimes, I visited the cafes near the shop to collect surplus food (for example, unsold sandwiches and hot pies); sometimes, I drove the shop van to the local community gardens to gather fresh vegetables. I had many other opportunities to engage with the reality of food surplus and witness how this community[4] is self-organized around the idea of 'not letting anyone go hungry'. My tasks included arranging the donated food in the aisles, cleaning the shop, saving edible potatoes, attending social events that raised awareness about food waste (such as volunteer nights, movie screenings and the celebration of the anniversary of the Free Food Store) and meeting with other volunteers and customers. When the shop

---

[3]   To protect the confidentiality of the shop manager, the pseudonym John is used.

[4]   The community included staff, volunteers, and those who visited the shop.

was open to customers, according to the weekly rotations, I welcomed them at the door, helped them get cold or hot food and, for simple accounting purposes, before they exited the shop I recorded the number of food items they took (see Chapter 2). Due to my ethical and political responsibilities as a researcher, I wanted to keep Mary informed about my findings and facilitate the participation of other organizational members in my study as much as possible. Still, there was neither an official agreement on nor an explicit expectation about how my research would be of value to the organization, other than the fact that I was offering my 'labour' as part of my research time. While I shared a common role with other volunteers, I also had access to organizational members for informal conversation.

Since 'much of the intriguing "mystery" of organizational life is hidden in the ordinary exchanges of ordinary people on an ordinary sort of day' (Ybema et al, 2009, p 1), I wanted to look through this ordinary-ness of daily practices and unravel social relations. In my first week, Mary introduced me to the other volunteers, and community members were made aware that I was doing volunteer work as a part of my research – my information sheet was posted on the announcements board. I explained to all colleagues working on the shift that I was researching alternative organizations, though I noted immediately that this would not mean much to many of them.

The discussions in this book rely on three sources of data – primary data in the form of field notes and from interviews, and secondary data from materials such as organizational documents and news articles. The first source, my field notes, were from my participant observation of the shop's daily operation. I kept a diary of my daily observations and my attendance at formal and informal gatherings. The second source, the interviews, were with ten volunteers the Free Food Store, who were from different age groups and had different experience levels (see the Appendix). Notably, some volunteers were also customers, so they provided views from both sides.[5] The interviews were semi-structured and took one to two hours. Through these interviews, I aimed to understand the position of the Free Food Store in the lives of the volunteers, their daily practices, how they perceived food surplus and the social relations at the Free Food Store, and their motivation for volunteering at the shop. I also had the opportunity to interview Mary and John, and, thanks to the Mary's assistance, representatives from three leading retailers that donated food regularly to the shop. All the interviews were recorded with participants' consent, and the interviewees were given assurances regarding confidentiality of their identity. The third

---

[5]   My volunteer role at the Free Food Store led to limited interaction with customers. Hence, my insights regarding customers are based on my observations of their visits to the shop and my relationship with those volunteers who were also customers.

source, secondary documents associated with the Free Food Store, included organizational documents, newsletters and news articles published in local newspapers. These helped me see how the Free Food Store communicated with its stakeholders and how it related to its own community.[6]

Following Timmermans and Tavory (2012, p 180), I drew on abductive reasoning to structure my data and findings. I maintained a dialogue between my empirical findings and the available theoretical frameworks to explain social phenomena so that I could develop my theoretical repertoire. As a part of this process, I neither tested a hypothesis through a hypo-deductive approach nor developed a new theory through an inductive approach. Instead, I gave primacy to the empirical world (that is, the journey of the food, the daily practices; see Van Maanen et al, 2007, p 1149). The more I engaged with the Free Food Store and gathered data, the more possibilities emerged to explain the social complexity around the shop. Discussions about the ontology of economic difference within the diverse economies framework (Gibson-Graham, 2008; Healy, 2009; Burke and Shear, 2014) and my focus on the organizational level of analysis guided my theoretical and analytical choices. Given my continuous questioning about the reason for the existence of the Free Food Store as a puzzling setting where faith plays a vital role against the backdrop of a neoliberal national context (hence, the reference to organizing faith), a noncapitalist, non-monetized, non-commoditized organizational space amid capitalist dynamics, with the power relations in the free shop (hence, the reference to organizing freedom), I focused on unravelling social relations and their impact on organizational members and the organization as a whole.

Beginnings of fieldwork

In January 2015, I had my induction as a volunteer at the Free Food Store. When I arrived at the shop, it was already afternoon, and work in the shop had begun. People were busy. Some were inside the big fridge, arranging the food; others were tidying up around the shop. I was asked to wait for Mary , and meanwhile John introduced himself. Mary joined us, and John left. We sat on an old couch in the corner of the shop, under notice boards where news articles about the shop were hanging. I had taken a look while I waited, to see how the Free Food Store was presented in the news articles. Most of the articles were from when the shop began operating in 2011. The local council supported the initiative, and the articles conveyed that the city had welcomed the Free Food Store. There were also announcements about

---

[6] To keep the identity of the Free Food Store and those of organizational actors confidential, full references to news articles are not given.

the shop's sister project – a community garden. During my induction, Mary informed me about the history of the Free Food Store, which had started out by taking small steps. She also told me of its objectives and how things were organized generally.

While I was very enthusiastic about starting my fieldwork, the procedural aspect of research had felt like a hassle (negotiating access, formalizing the ethics'approval application, structuring the information sheet, keeping Mary informed about the start date and so on). It did not become a significant issue thanks to Mary's understanding and tolerance. She let me know I could hang my information sheet on one of the notice boards, letting others know about the purpose of my research at the Free Food Store. After the induction, I completed the volunteer form and was officially part of the organization. My fieldwork had begun!

Vignette: A typical day in the shop

In the middle of the city, the Free Food Store is opening for the day. When I enter the shop in the morning, I notice the radio is already on: the radio station The Breeze is playing a popular song. It's a lovely start to the day with the music, and it feels comforting to see John, who has become a friend to me since I started my volunteer work. My day begins with a quick welcome chit-chat with John, and then, following the arrival of other volunteers, we get to work. I start my usual task of restocking the fridge and arranging the food stored there (mostly yoghurt; sometimes dips, if there is a big enough donation). (On days when there is no food, I clean the refrigerator.) Then I organize the food collected from various retailers and cafes during the day, which arrives at the shop at different times; this can include many loaves of bread and significant amounts of vegetables, fruits, herbs, canned food and various kinds of sweets.

The shop seems empty in the morning but volunteers fill the shelves with (surplus) food, ready to open for customers between 4.30 pm and 6.00 pm. I volunteer every Thursday, doing the morning and evening shifts, each with different priorities and responsibilities. It's Thursday, so, as happens on this day each week, 400 kilograms of potatoes is delivered in a trailer; along with other volunteers, I select the edible ones among the close to rotten, box them and carry them into the shop. Then, in the shop, we make up packages for customers (three kilograms of potatoes per package).

Up to 3.00 pm, we organize the aisles and do the cleaning. At 4.00 pm, the evening shift begins, with a new round of volunteers, who all prepare straight away to serve the food to customers. While the hot food coming from the cafes is kept warm, cold sandwiches have their place in the fridge. The line of customers in front of the shop starts forming around 3.30 pm, and after ten minutes of 'grab time' for volunteers at 4.20 pm, the doors open to everyone, without any restriction, at 4.30 pm. The Free Food Store is free and accessible to all. Based on the amount of 'saved' surplus food that is available, the director of the shop makes an announcement at the front of the shop that the customers can have hot (for example, pies, sausage rolls, other savoury foods) and cold (for example, fresh sandwiches, muffins, scones) food (on other days, they have to choose one option). After 6.00 pm, other community organizations in the area collect the leftover food (mostly loaves of bread).

After a few days of volunteering, I had a general overview of the workings of the Free Food Store. Many businesses, including local cafes, donate surplus food, but the bulk of the donations come from local branches of national food retailers and food wholesalers. They donate food either daily – for food that has gone past its expiry date – or occasionally – for non-marketable, but still edible, food products that have been mislabelled or which have quality issues. The food is usually collected using the Free Food Store van and volunteers' cars, or businesses delivered bulk donations (for example, kilograms of yoghurt or dips) in their trucks. Fresh vegetables and fruits are sometimes available from community gardens and are occasionally donated by individuals.

After arrival, food belongs to the Free Food Store, to be given with 'unconditional love'. Terms like 'unconditional giving' and 'unconditional love' are used on notices around the Free Food Store and in its organizational documents. These represent Mary's spirituality and, by extension, the organization's identity. The donated food needs to be packaged or divided into small amounts by volunteers so that as many people as possible can get a wide variety of food. Small loaves of bread are bundled; packs of muffins packs are opened, to be served individually; and teabags are divided out. This process also includes scoring out the barcodes of packaged foods to prevent returns or resales to retailers. While John oversees the shop's operations, volunteers are involved in their various tasks. After waiting in the queue outside the shop, customers come inside and choose the food they want.

At the end of the day, after the amount of food items provided to each customer is recorded, the exchange process is over, and the food belongs to a very diverse group of customers (for example, families, young couples, students, people who are homeless and older people), who take it back home (if they have one). If there is still food left, other local organizations pick it up from the shop and distribute it elsewhere.

In terms of operating hours, the work of the Free Food Store begins at 11.00 am and ends at 6.00 pm. The work day is divided into two shifts, each with assigned volunteers. However, due to the nature of voluntary work, turnover is high, and the volunteers marked down for shifts often change – I see a lot of different faces during my shifts. During the day shift

(11.00 am to 3.00 pm), the work is mainly handling the arrival of food. The evening shift (4.00 pm to 6.00 pm) is explicitly timed so as not to conflict with the business hours of local cafes. During this shift, the work is packaging and shelving fresh food before customers enter the shop, then serving the donated food to customers.

Each volunteer has a specific role in the evening shift, assigned just before the shop opens to customers – they might be welcoming people at the door, serving cold food from the fridge, organizing the fruit and vegetable section for the convenience of customers, giving out the hot food that comes in from local cafes or recording the amount of food provided per customer. Recording the food is like bookkeeping for the day and keeps the Free Food Store accountable to the board of trustees and the community.

The amount of fresh food that's available varies depending on what the suppliers (that is, retailers and cafes) provide on the day – there might be more than 20 cold sandwiches on one day but only three or four scones on another. At 4.20 pm, the ten-minute grab time for volunteers on the evening shift starts; during this time, they can take whatever they choose before the shop opens to customers. Following grab time, the volunteers, John and Mary come together. This is the time when Mary shares what things are happening at the Free Food Store and, with the participation of others, prays and thanks God for the food, the volunteers and the customers.

Complex social relations bring this small charity shop to life and mobilize volunteers, and these provide insights regarding the economic practices producing poverty amid abundance. In addition to its alternative economic form (discussed later), the very existence of the Free Food Store is already a signifier of ongoing socioeconomic challenges in the area. Despite all the difficulties it addresses, the shop also gives hope for imagining alternatives based on the organizing potential of communities. Therefore, the shop provides an interesting organizational case that makes invisible, complex and messy relations visible.

The Free Food Store is more than a food bank

Given the Free Food Store's business model – based on collecting surplus food from retailers and redistributing it, relying on volunteer labour – and the disadvantaged profile of customers, it has some essential similarities with the role of food banks, and other food charities, in developed countries (Escajedo et al, 2017). These similarities shed light on the complex economic environment in which such food rescue organizations operate. For instance, like food banks, the Free Food Store, as a charity shop, can be considered a Band-Aid solution to the structural issue of poverty (Poppendieck, 1998) and a means of depoliticizing food poverty against the background of a neoliberal society (Riches, 2011; Watson, 2019).

These sorts of organization are criticized on the basis that their practices may lead to shame and stigma for beneficiaries, and because they have potential to host paternalistic power relations (Garthwaite, 2016; Caraher and Furey, 2018). Furthermore, traditionally, food banks have close ties and formal links with different churches and faith groups (Salonen, 2016; Power et al, 2017).

On the other hand, the perishable nature of the food and lack of restrictions on who can benefit are key aspects of the Free Food Store that make it quite different from typical food banks. These aspects are seen as community innovations to improve well-being and transform power relations (Watson, 2019). Moreover, although the Free Food Store is registered legally as a charity, it does not sell anything like some other charity stores and is not linked with a specific faith group or church. It made three formal applications before being registered as a charity – not setting any restrictions on who could benefit from the shop worked against the application, as the regulator perceived that the Free Food Store did not perform charity work for people who were in need. For the Free Food Store, the aim of gaining registration as a charity was to have a legal and official status that would allow them to interact effectively with stakeholders and help benefactors get tax deductions based on their donations. Given the shop's relations with retailers and cafes, it is inevitably connected to market dynamics, but as far as its own operation goes, there is no monetary exchange. The surplus food, including perishable items from retailers and community gardens, is given free to anyone, with no criteria limiting who can benefit.

While some commentators acknowledge the limitations of such initiatives and the need for more structural solutions, they also emphasize the importance of doing something positive concerning food surplus 'right here, right now' – something that will care for the natural environment and empower communities (Dey and Humphries, 2015; Diprose and Lee, 2022). Hence, as Watson (2019) argues, the food rescue ecosystem is complex and contradictory. While it enables food waste to be rescued and meets people's needs, it also relies on and supports the same system that normalizes food poverty and charity-based solutions (Watson, 2019, p 81). This contradictory context must be taken into account when trying to understand the Free Food Store's role and function as an alternative organization.

The vision of the Free Food Store is 'to be a community that won't let anyone go hungry' (free food store documents), thus arguably problematizing food poverty, while its mission is to 'rescue surplus food and help those in need' (free food store documents), which implies a social mission. Mary's role is to communicate with stakeholders, act as a spokesperson, find funding for the operation, network and, provide moral and ideological leadership. She is a member of the shop's board of trustees and accountable to the board. The presence of the board is hardly felt by volunteers, since they primarily interact with John in his role as shop manager, and Mary tends to be out doing her work. John is in charge of arranging the volunteers' workload and preparing their weekly schedules, as well as managing the daily operation of the shop. He opens and closes the shop and is the contact person during the day for occasional food donations or deliveries to other community organizations. The director and manager are paid part-time employees of the organization, but they work full-time at the shop, essentially doing part-time volunteer work on top of their paid roles. Volunteers, who provide their free labour, have a diverse profile, including Pākehā (New Zealanders of European descent), Māori, international residents, people with disabilities, students, academics, pensioners, people who are unemployed and professionals. During my fieldwork, there were 60 volunteers working at the shop. According to the shop's own figures as of September 2023, since the shop's opening in December 2011, the total number of people who have volunteered has reached approximately 100, and the average number of customers per day has increased from 85 to 325. This demonstrates the rising demand for the Free Food Store due to increasing food poverty in (post-)pandemic conditions. While the shop is open to all and welcomes diversity, it has its own power relations and political dynamics, which are the topic of Chapter 5.

The general trend is that many volunteers come to the shop first as customers, and as they learn more about the shop, they become volunteers. Word of mouth and publicity in local newspapers also bring many volunteers to the shop. The only privilege associated with being a volunteer is that on days when you work in the shop, you can take what you need before the shop opens. The volunteers occasionally come together for social or fundraising events, contributing to the community feeling around the shop. I had the opportunity to attend a couple of these events.

At first glance, the Free Food Store does not appear to be a Christian organization per se. Apart from some notes on the notice board, no visible artefacts or symbols reflecting religious statements are present. Still, the driving values of the director have strong associations with religious discourse – she has Christian beliefs and she worked for Christian food banks before founding the shop. This association with faith influences the shop's mission in terms of giving unconditionally to the community. In addition, some volunteers are driven by faith and make sense of their involvement at the shop through religious discourse. The role of faith and religion in organizing the Free Food Store is discussed in depth in Chapter 3.

As an organizational model based on rescuing surplus food and giving it away for free in a shop setting, the Free Food Store presents an interesting case of a needs-based alternative economy – it mimics other food shops where customers can come and pick up whatever they want, within reasonable limits; but there is no money involved, the director and shop manager have limited wage relations (dependent on donations and grants), volunteers maintain the shop, fresh produce is donated by retailers and picked up from community gardens, and anyone regardless of their income and assets can visit the shop to get food. There are other food rescue organizations similar to the Free Food Store in Aotearoa New Zealand. Still, during my fieldwork, none were organized as a free shop where people (that is, anyone) can come and pick up food (see Mirosa et al, 2016). The organization's website indicates that the Free Food Store is the longest-running free shop and a pioneer, inspiring other shops in different cities.

The Free Food Store as a case of an alternative-substitute institution

In this context, Fuller and Jonas' (2003) conceptualization of 'alternative-substitute' institutions explains the alterity of the Free Food Store compared to food banks and other charity-based solutions. Alternative-substitute institutions are a substitute for those which no longer exist, and are considered a last resort. While these organizations may not aim to be an alternative to dominant (economic) practices, they can be regarded as a coping mechanism of communities at local scale (Fuller and Jonas, 2003, pp 57–58) and offer an infrastructure for socially useful production and doing (Chatterton and Pusey, 2020). As needs-driven organizations, they rely on sharing or gift economies, have cooperative labour relations and host alternative value relations (Jonas, 2013, p 34). The role of the Free Food Store as an alternative organization amid capitalist economic relations is discussed in Chapter 4.

Various groups in the community support the Free Food Store. For instance, after leaving its former site at a petrol station, the city council granted it access to a new building, and the cost of fitting this out, around NZ$100,000, was covered by donations and support from numerous businesses and community members (news article). Local political figures, high school students and business people visit the Free Food Store and promote volunteering among the community (news article). The shop won the Not for Profit Award at the prestigious local business awards in 2022. Additionally, the Free Food Store has a positive image in the community, based on its aim of raising awareness about food waste.

The rescued surplus food circulates twice after coming to the shop. Donated food is first taken by the shop's customers (including the volunteers). Then, at the end of the day, the leftovers are collected by other local and regional charities or community organizations. It can be argued that the Free Food Store mediates an alternative distribution network (see Figure 1.1).

Figure 1.1: The Free Food Store as an alternative food distribution channel

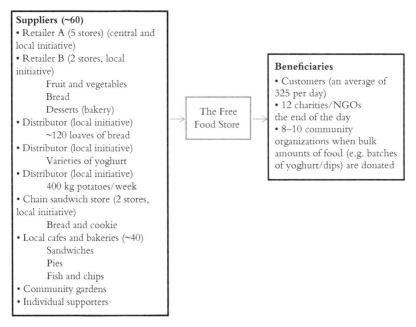

Source: The Free Food Store's figures as of September 2023

To conclude this chapter, as a side note – but a critical one – I would point out that my study was conducted before the COVID-19 pandemic. During the pandemic, according to the shop's social media account, they played a critical role – similar to other food rescue initiatives (Clare et al, 2023). They continued to provide surplus food, sometimes in coordination with other food banks. In a social media post from October 2021, the shop announced the need for growth and restructuring in response to the pandemic conditions. The post noted the shop's huge rise in activities over the past couple of years due to two things: first, the fact pandemic conditions had led to increased attention on where food comes from and the importance of avoiding waste in food industries and hospitality, thus leading to more food rescue; and, second, the increase in numbers of people looking for help to access food.

However, in October and November 2022, they were affected by food shortages due to the disruptions in the global food supply chain that impacted retailers donating food. They posted at this point that because of shortages, they were having to restrict the amount of food they could offer. They noted that this had been a difficult decision and asked for customers' understanding.

A more recent post, from September 2023, stated that they were serving an average of 325 people and distributing 1,300 kilograms of food on a daily basis.

2

In Search of Alternatives across the Bridge

While the Free Food Store might be considered a marginal organizational actor in the context of the global food system, for me it provided an entry point for critical questions about food. It also brought up questions about my role within the organization, as an academic. In this chapter, I introduce the big picture concerning the mobilization around food surplus and then share my initial reflections and questions. As I argue throughout the book, the Free Food Store is more than a charity shop operating primarily for the benefit of the local community at the centre of a town. Its existence provides an opportunity to ask questions about the role of faith in organizing, poverty amid abundance and the limits of freedom in a community organization.

Seeing the big picture

According to the World Food Programme (2023), 'as many as 783 million people are facing chronic hunger' due to various reasons, such as conflict, climate change and increasing production costs. While they identify hunger hot spots 'from the Central American Dry Corridor and Haiti, through the Sahel, Central African Republic, South Sudan and then eastwards to the Horn of Africa, Syria, Yemen and all the way to Afghanistan' (World Food Programme, 2023), according to a recent Food and Agriculture Organization report, the share of the population facing hunger in 2022[1] was 19.7 per cent in Africa, 8.5 per cent in Asia, 7.0 per cent in Oceania and 6.5 per cent in Latin America and the Caribbean. The share for Northern America and Europe was less than 2.5 per cent (Food and Agriculture Organization et al, 2023, Table 1). The same report provides figures on the prevalence of moderate or severe food insecurity in the total population from the period

---

[1]   Figures are based on mid-year estimates.

2014–2016 to the period 2020–2022: despite the relatively positive findings for Global North countries (there was a slight decrease in Western Europe, from 5.2 per cent to 4.9 per cent; in the UK, the share fell from 6.3 per cent to 4.1 per cent), the prevalence increased in Aotearoa New Zealand (from 10.0 per cent to 15.1 per cent), Australia (from 10.8 per cent to 11.4 per cent) and Japan (from 2.6 per cent to 4.4 per cent) (Food and Agriculture Organization et al, 2023, Table A1.1).

Nevertheless, in the UK, according to The Trussell Trust (2023), a national food bank network, three million emergency food parcels were distributed between April 2022 and March 2023 – the most parcels ever distributed by the network in a single financial year, including at the height of the COVID-19 pandemic. In Canada, a similar trend can be seen, with food bank use in March 2023 indicating: 'a 32 per cent increase compared to March 2022, and a 78.5 per cent increase compared to March 2019' (Food Banks Canada, 2023). Radio New Zealand (2023) reports that 'hundreds of thousands' of Kiwis in working families struggling to secure sufficient food, due to (post-)pandemic conditions and the rising cost of living, are turning to food banks for support.

What do all these numbers say to you, my dear reader? Setting aside the historical and structural inequalities leading to food insecurity in the Global South, there are many people living in so-called 'developed countries' who cannot afford food even when they are in employment. This situation makes the amount of food waste even more of a burning issue at global level.

Popular media (Stuart, 2009; Woolf, 2020) and academic research (Campbell et al, 2017; Huang et al, 2020) increasingly raise social, ethical, environmental and economic concerns regarding the amount of food surplus that is becoming waste. Governments have enacted food donation laws forbidding wastage of surplus food and forcing retailers to donate it to charities,[2] and there is growing organizational mobilization at different scales to deal with surplus food and food waste (Vlaholias et al, 2015). However, there is a striking discrepancy between the amount of surplus food that exists and the levels of food poverty. While around 800 million people are affected by hunger globally in 2021 according to the FAO report (2023), 'around 931 million tonnes of food waste was generated in 2019' – the equivalent of 17 per cent of total global food production – through households, the food service industry and retail outlets (United Nations Environment Programme, 2021, p 8). The simultaneous existence of large-scale waste and widespread food poverty is an alarming indication of global inequality. And then there is also the impact waste is having on climate change.

---

[2]   See the Global Food Donation Policy Atlas: atlas.foodbanking.org

While addressing this discrepancy at both consumer and commercial levels has emerged as a prominent concern, our deeply ingrained economic relationships and structural barriers pose substantial challenges to systemic change (Böhm et al, 2020). As a part of the mobilization around surplus food, it has been common practice for many businesses to donate the food they cannot sell so that it can be distributed to those who are in need (Alexander and Smaje, 2008; Warshawsky, 2016). It is argued that this has a significant role to play in reducing food waste and fighting food insecurity. However, questions have been raised as to the extent to which these aims can be achieved using this approach, since it is considered a short-term solution that offers beneficiaries nutritionally limited food and support that is undignified. At a broader level, food banks and food charities have become signifiers of poverty, lack of food justice and the limits of the neoliberal economic system (Escajedo San-Epifanio et al, 2017). They are considered Band-Aid solutions that normalize and depoliticize food poverty (Caplan, 2017). Despite their best intentions, they cannot confront the structural aspects of food poverty and related societal questions, such as how to organize the 'redistribution of food' (Poppendieck, 1998; Szende, 2015). The problem of food surplus, food waste and food poverty persists and creates a challenge not only for these sorts of organization but also for social movements, governments and universities considering the social consequences of (economic) inequality (Holt-Giménez, 2019).

Nevertheless, it is also argued that such efforts can make a difference to and create social value for stakeholder groups and communities (Mirosa et al, 2016). Despite their limitations, these needs-based organizations with an alternative moral economy offer new opportunities to rethink food, community and economic relations. On the one hand, the Free Food Store takes on the burden of what the state and private sector should be doing – that is, meeting the needs of society through a living wage and affordable prices. On the other hand, initiatives like the Free Food Store are interpreted in multiple other ways – they are seen as tackling food poverty, offering sustainable food networks, supporting self-organizing communities, managing retailers' surpluses and meeting community needs.

Thus, the issue we see here has multiple layers: a global food chain organized on the premise of low cost with direct impact on greenhouse emissions; lack of (humane) welfare mechanisms that protect citizens from the operation of market forces; and a civic network that is organized according to either lifestyle choice or religious background. The Free Food Store plays a minor role against the backdrop of this multilevel complexity. A critical perspective would complicate analysis of the issue by considering how solutions such as the Free Food Store contribute to the social reproduction of labour – through the free shop, food is always available, and this enables people to go to work the next day instead of problematizing the structural conditions of food poverty they experience. Analyzing the complexity at hand also leads us to ask questions about the economic value of surplus food and food waste (Evans et al, 2012), and the role of actors in surplus food redistribution (Warshawsky, 2016).

Mary, the founder/director of the Free Food Store, takes a positive view on the complexity of these relations: "It may be a fatalistic view, but instead of looking at what we can't do, we've been looking at what we can do with the [Free Food Store]." The question then is how the Free Food Store emerged as a community organization and what I can learn from it as a critical organization scholar. As ethnographic researchers will know, there are no easy answers to these sorts of question. In the next section, a comment from a colleague at the Free Food Store leads to many questions, with many possible answers, concerning the shop and the academic who intends to make sense of what is happening.

You are different! Am I?

"You are not like others, those who stay on the other side of the bridge and do their jobs as academics. You cross the bridge, come here and work with us. You are different." This is what I was told by a colleague at the Free Food Store when we were splitting bulk food packages into small batches for distribution to customers. By referring to the university's location on the other side of the bridge, on the city's outskirts, my friend eloquently expressed her perception of academics. This is not a new debate, for sure; for decades, academics have been asked about their relevance and how they make an impact, or the extent to which they can touch people's lives with the knowledge they produce. Meanwhile, they are expected to continuously perform through publishing, and the value of their scholarship is assessed by higher education managers on this narrow basis. It has become much more difficult to 'cross the bridge' and act beyond the confines of 'the university'. So, thinking about what my friend told me in daily conversation, how challenging it is to be put into such a position, and am I really different? The situation I found myself in was not peculiar or unique, as many other academics have been confronted with such comments and have faced the challenging tension between the academy and activism. However, in writing about my experience in this book, I wonder if I have imagined/represented/constructed an alternative self? Is this the tension between my academic-self and activist-self, expressed throughout this book?

Inevitably, the dialogue between the academic and the activist selves goes like this: Is it enough to cross the bridge – to go into the field and work with communities – and then report in the form of journal articles that pile up in libraries or offices? Is this the critical impact I can create as an academic? On the other hand, can I really create a bridge between activism and scholarship? Given my privilege – having access to millions of sources of knowledge while continually accruing more knowledge – can I harness those resources to be of use to the community organizations I engage with? Would the community organizations be interested in knowing what I study, and why I study it, and consider me a resource? Perhaps the answer ultimately lies in burning the bridge and leaving behind the academy's old-fashioned rituals and imposed traditions. How about reimagining a new academy, or way of academic working, alongside communities and, more importantly, with an activist orientation, leading to new opportunities and tensions? How can I (re)imagine myself as an academic activist despite the challenges of crossing the bridge? With this ebb and flow of academic-activist tension through the fractured persona, can there be a resolution?

Well, why not think, write and act differently through embodied experiences, aspirations and imaginations (Prichard and Benschop, 2018; Pullen, 2018)? This is not an easy effort, though. Being conditioned for years to produce knowledge in certain ways (through, shall I say, the discourse of the university, with a nod to Lacan (2007)), I could not help but ask at the very outset of writing this text: Do I need to justify this as an academic effort or not (Ruth et al, 2018)? Do I need to think strategically about who and what to cite (Parker and Thomas, 2011; Butler and Spoelstra, 2014)? Do I have a right to occupy an academic book chapter with my own scholarly informed activist musings and tensions? Am I using 'I' too much? Or should I just let it go and see where I end up? Can this book be considered an activist text calling academics to action?

Sorry for posing so many questions, but I guess, my dear reader, you already feel the uneasiness flowing from this text – an academic trying to be an activist, trying to cast off his institutional chains, aiming to unfold the tensions of being in the field with a critical agenda and multiple roles, but also trying to write a chapter in an academic book in an unconventional way. Does this mean I crossed the bridge but came back to write this text differently? You are right; the whole text is an effort to respond to these unending questions and make sense of the tensions between the academic-self and the activist-self. Are you with me? Sorry – another question. Academic habits die hard! Let's move on.

Questions, queries, reflections

This is me (Figure 2.1), happily carrying some fresh vegetables from the shop van to the Free Food Store. Yes, that's right – the food is free here. The shop is located in the Manawatu Region of Aotearoa New Zealand. It gives surplus food (which the shop refers to as 'rescued food' – that is, rescued from becoming waste) without any monetary exchange. It is like the usual sort of shop, but you do not pay for the food you get. It is unique, with many layers of complexity, and it does not fit the typical organizational

Figure 2.1: Me carrying fresh produce

forms we know about. It is not a food bank, where you would be asked to justify your access to food through some form of means-testing. (Isn't it awful that you can be asked to formalize your own poverty to get some food?) Besides that, depending on donations, perishable food such as yoghurt, fish or dips are available in the shop – this also makes it different from food banks, which exclusively stock nonperishable food items. These differences from food banks attract people to the Free Food Store. This is very broadly what I study as an academic: How can a place like the Free Food Store be possible today? Is it genuinely free? What kind of organizational form does it represent? Can I untangle the layers of complexity in this bottom–up community organization problematizing food waste? Do we see in this place alternative engagement by the community and for the community? Yet, for me, as an academic with activist aspirations, the big questions are: How can I take this further? Can I challenge the structural dynamics of food waste and food poverty? And if I can, in what ways? Perhaps these aims are too ambitious, to be fair. Am I able to cross the bridge?

A wide variety of food is donated to the shop. For instance, once a week, 400 kilograms of potatoes are delivered – the potatoes are saved from becoming waste, and are mostly rotten and awfully stinky (see Figure 2.2). As discussed in Chapter 1, on my first day as a volunteer, and beginning my research, at the Free Food Store, a container full of potatoes was dumped at the door of the shop. Volunteers were asked to pick the good ones and

Figure 2.2: Picking edible potatoes

then box and store them. The potatoes would then be bagged for the customers coming in the evening. It was a seemingly easy task; however, the challenge was to pick good, edible potatoes. The quality of a good potato is all about texture, smell and look. One by one, as I dug into the mountain of potatoes, I first checked the feel of the potato – was it hard enough, not cracked, with a relatively smooth surface? Then, there would come the smell and visual quality control. I would put a potato in the box if it was not smelly and looked generally OK. However, picking up good ones also meant dealing with the mushy, stinky rotten ones, which obviously was not a pleasant experience. That is why we used disposable gloves. Still, gloves did not make much difference as I bent over the container, next to a colleague, fighting with the potato mountain to capture the good ones and trying to avoid any mud, dirt and sticky mushiness, the smell hitting my face. It is hard to describe the transformation of potatoes, normally beloved as fries.

Nevertheless, perhaps, this was when my hands, face and body got dirty as an academic in this context – getting dirty, dusty and stinky while picking the good potatoes that would be food on people's tables. Frankly, I was worried that it would be the same every week. Fortunately, the following week, the potatoes were not as rotten and stinky as they were that first week.

Our task is to take the good, edible ones; the rest go to the pigs. Tom – the old Māori chap who delivered the potatoes in a huge container – told a joke about one of the pigs becoming so huge that it was capable of eating a child. Legends of pigs chasing kids in the farms of Manawatu – not a bad start for my participatory research – that's what I was thinking that day, as I boxed and bagged the edible potatoes for those who would come to the shop that evening.

Figure 2.3: Dozens of loaves and other bread products

Edible potatoes? Edible vegetables? What kind of quality is edible? Do we think about edibility when we shop for food at the supermarket? Do we ever consider why the fruit and vegetables we see on supermarket shelves have near flawless colour and shape? What happens to bananas that are too short or too long, or how about those large, greenish tomatoes that we used to see in grandma's garden but don't find in supermarkets? I cannot help but ask: Are supermarkets the Disneyland of food where we only see the shiny and perfect (mis)representation of the (capitalist) world? You can have everything you want – fresh, with various bright colours, produced and packaged just today (God bless freedom of choice!) – but only so long as you have enough money to pay for it. For a long time now, when shopping I have found myself thinking about the potato's origin, production process and qualities. Isn't it surprising that we are so obsessed with the qualities of food, but we mostly neglect its journey from the field to the fork, or in my case to the landfill? Do you also feel this alienation when healthy food is not a right anymore, but a commodity?

Bread, dozens of loaves of bread! Shelves full of bread with different brands and with a variety of ingredients. Basic, fancy, gourmet! (See Figures 2.3 and 2.4.) Precisely at their expiry date, they are donated. Why on earth would we produce such an amount of bread? Do we really consume so much of it? If the Free Food Store did not exist, this expired bread would be dumped in a landfill or become a feast for the pigs. Oh wait; thousands of people in Aotearoa New Zealand cannot access food regularly.

Something is going wrong here, seriously. Aotearoa New Zealand is a country based on primary industries and agriculture; it is a country of food. So why, then, are there so many people coming to the Free Food Store?

Figure 2.4: More bread

Can't they afford food? Who are they, these customers coming to the shop every day – the poor, people who are homeless, those who cannot balance their budget or cannot make it to the end of the month, those who are on welfare, those with many kids, those who have mental health issues, those who find the shop convenient and pop in for a sandwich? Though the customers are different from one another, they are all people of the town who have likely been through similar challenges and hardships of life and need additional support. The Free Food Store does not make distinctions. 'Unconditional love' and 'unconditional giving' – these are the shop's mottos. Wealthy or poor, whoever or whatever you are, you can get food from the shop. No judgement at all (even if you drive a fancy car or wear a nice suit). No means-testing either. So, who or what am I here? An academic who has been perplexed by the amount of surplus food that would typically go to waste and has become angry at the social and economic inequality he has been brought face to face with. Through my activist-self, can I fight inequality from this tiny shop?

It is the so-called 'grab time' for volunteers, the ten-minute time slot after the shelves are sorted and volunteers can choose whatever they want – it is the shop's way of saying thank you to volunteers (see Chapter 1). In my case, it is always a complicated time, and I find myself having the same inner dialogue, along the lines of: There's a sandwich that looks pretty delicious, but should I have it? Why not – I'm a volunteer here; I put in my labour for today and it's my right to have a sandwich. No, I shouldn't; I can generally afford one of those sandwiches from a cafe; I have a regular and relatively high salary as an academic. I should leave it to those who really need it. Come on; it's only a sandwich! But look at the other volunteers – they take more than one item. Why not a sandwich as a reward for the day? Labour in exchange for food seems like a good deal, but then, is it free food?

While I question my motive and struggle with my multiple roles at the shop, grab time has already been and gone. Time to note the amounts of the food items we, the volunteers, are taking from the shop.

Following grab time, Mary comes into the shop. We all gather next to the counter, and she gives a five-minute update with news from the shop and a motivational talk, then holds a joint prayer – "Thank God the store has amazing volunteers and suppliers." Indeed, it is all about volunteer labour. How can we value free labour here? The ethnographer in my head reminds me I need to note down what's happening: collecting food from retailers and cafes, sorting them, arranging shelves, cleaning the shop and delivering the food. More than 60 volunteers, coming and going on routine shifts.

"Word of mouth brings people here", says Alex,[3] one of the volunteers, in an interview. I wonder whether it is a case of the community finding its own way to fight food poverty and help each other. My activist-self keeps asking: is this enough? While we are all surrounded by an economic system that produces surplus food and food poverty, where do our limits begin and end in terms of our agency, our intervention? This initiative is praiseworthy, since it does not let surplus food go to waste. Yet how are we to think of fair and just redistribution of food or, more importantly, wealth? Perhaps, it is all about food sovereignty as a force to challenge the corporate food regime. Can I create time within the shop's daily routine to talk about these issues with other volunteers? Would they be interested in listening to me? I am afraid they would get bored with all the jargon I am used to using, despite my enthusiastic political speech, and it would end with the typical Kiwi way of declining the offer, something like: 'Yeah, naaaah mate, better we sort out the food issue, eh?' Stuck between my academic-self (who would like to understand this place and people) and my activist-self (who would like to engage with the cause and ask for more mobilization), I wonder: Is there a way we can find common ground for social change, for fair redistribution of food and wealth? Is this only on *my* agenda, as a part of an academic exercise?

Praying? Not my cup of tea, and apparently it is not for some of the other volunteers either. Yet we stand together with all due respect. No need to be religious to be here, but you feel its influence; it is in the air – the idea of unconditional love and giving, and the collaboration of people from religious communities, fostered through word of mouth at different churches. Is benevolent Christianity the answer to the inequalities of this society? Can unconditional love stand face to face with and even triumph over market demands? Should I return to liberation theology's principles or

---

[3]   Alex is a pseudonym used to protect the confidentiality of the volunteer.

Walter Benjamin's discussions about theology and historical materialism using the puppet metaphor?[4] (My academic-self notes this down in my journal.) What kind of actions might radicalize and politicize such an effort so that the community may also ask whether this is enough? (My activist-self poses this question.) On the other hand, perhaps, I have no ground at all here. Who am I to push the boundaries for the people who come here because of various needs? What am I to them? (This is what my anxious self asks.)

The shop is open! I am standing at the door; customers are waiting to get inside. Families with kids have priority, so I welcome them first. Mary goes out to the front of the shop and talks through a loudspeaker before letting people in: "You may have one warm and cold tonight, folks." This is code for the availability of fresh food – sandwiches, pies, hot dogs, fish and chips, any other leftovers from the cafes on the day. Not so fortunate every day, though – sometimes there are only some sandwiches. Once things get going, I check how long the line at the counter is – if not too long, I let some more customers in.

I hold out the coin donation box – though the customers don't need to donate. A few coins are given from time to time. My hunch tells me that donating just a few dollars makes customers feel much more comfortable about being there. It is already difficult for some of them to stand in a queue or to be seen queuing up for 'free food'. Visibility of people queuing just outside the shop is a topic of discussion, and we are asked to smile at them and not be judgmental. I am not judgmental, but I worry about the kids with bare feet running around on this winter day, and I am concerned about the older people who come here every day, and I wonder about the life of the young couple with four kids. This diversity of customers tells me that life has not been easy for many and that often people are simply trying their best to make it to the end of the month. No, I am not judgmental at all; in fact, I am very much angry at the conditions that impoverish people's lives and do not let them have any other option than the Free Food Store to get some decent food. Can my academic-self let me be angry?

While volunteers freely share their manual labour, customers bring their emotional labour, which is not easy to practice, in the form of feelings of shame: 'I am waiting in the queue outside this shop, visible to the entire city, hoping to get inside to get free food. People will know I need free food.' This is a topic I discussed with many of the community members – while

---

[4]   Here, I purposefully refer to two distinct sources about the role of religious faith in social transformation. Liberation theology is a Christian religious movement that has been influential in Latin America, addressing socio-economic injustices and promoting active political participation to change oppressive structures through religious faith. In the other reference, I remind Walter Benjamin's critique of historical materialism and the role spirituality and theology can play in social change.

some customers seem confident and feel OK about getting food from the shop, others seem insecure and may feel a bit of shame for being at the shop. I can recall many first-time visitors to the shop who were hesitant to choose from the available food options, and many times over they thanked Mary and others. Despite the best intentions of the Free Food Store, I suppose this reflects the dark side of charity philosophy. Instead of being able to act as rights-based citizens, seeking a decent life through political struggle, many are put into a vulnerable position that becomes emotional labour for access to free food and moral discourse. This also makes me question whether those with no option but to sell their labour are in an advantageous position. Perhaps, regardless of our emotional or physical orientations, none of us is in a better situation. As we carry out different forms of labour, we have nothing to lose but the chains of capitalism suffocating us. Do I have the courage to lose my own chains in a highly casualized academy, especially given that I am the sole provider for my family?

Waiting at the shop door, feeling the wind and occasionally shaking the donation box, I note that there are regular customers too – familiar faces I see every week. Do they rely on the Free Food Store for their needs? It is not healthy at all, as much of the food available is high in carbohydrates and sugar. Occasionally, they can get yoghurt, milk and dips, and to some extent vegetables – yellowish broccoli and a bag of not-too-bad potatoes (see Figure 2.5). Fresh veggies are rarely available from the community gardens or the neighbourhood – only on lucky days.

Better to begin a chat while customers wait in the queue. Talk about the weather: "Cold, isn't it?" What else can I talk about? Challenges of being a non-native English speaker? I have difficulty initiating a conversation and

Figure 2.5: Fruit and vegetables

even greater difficulty understanding the customers' friendly jokes. That is not an easy task at all for me – should I call this another form of emotional labour, only this time performed by me? I smile as if I get a customer's joke. These are the uneasy moments of being a gatekeeper and letting people in. Smile, greet. Do not judge. Remember 'unconditional love'. They look at my eyes and check inside occasionally, wondering when I will let them in. When they enter the shop, they go to the fridges first, fruit and vegetables second, and then they are free to 'shop' in the other aisles. Another moment of questioning: What am I really doing here? Can I use these moments of encounter as an opportunity to know these people, as getting inside the shop seems to be the only thing on their minds? I better not forget to check if the other volunteers are doing OK as they deliver food from the fridges, give out yoghurts, sandwiches or larger food items to families, let customers choose between this cupcake and that muffin.

Many times as a volunteer I have been stationed beside the fridges, where customers spend much time if fresh food is abundant that day. A typical conversation between volunteers and customers would be:

Volunteer: Hi, how are you tonight? What can I get you? A chicken or beef sandwich?

Customer: What else do you have, mate? [Looks through the fridge window.]

Volunteer: Let me see. [Quickly checks to see what the other sandwiches are.] Cheese and onion, if you want?

Customer: Hmmm. [Pauses for ten seconds.]

Volunteer: How about chicken with mayo?

Customer: No, beef.

Volunteer: OK, here it is.

Similar dialogue takes place regarding the sweet stuff – muffins with berries or chocolate? (See Figure 2.6.) Next to a fridge, I am the guardian of the food this time. I need to be polite and responsive so that we distribute the food fairly and no one takes advantage of the abundance of food available this day. Who knows whether there will be sandwiches the next day? Customers can get multiple items if they come with their families to the shop, and most likely there will be someone sitting in the car or unable to get to the shop. I try not to judge but stay protective of the food – I would like to trust the customers and accept what they are telling me. The joy of the kids when they get food is incredible, though. Some ask for food with hesitation and pure excitement, while others ask timidly with a bit of shyness.

The shop expects that customers will take only as much as they need and that they will respect others. There are reminders about respecting

Figure 2.6: Sweet stuff

others (see Figure 2.7a), and volunteers oversee and control the amount of food customers get. In fact, the free shop can suddenly turn into a kind of 'big brother', watching those who enter. Only mild surveillance? Another emotional labour emerges for the customers too: they should be considerate of the food they get from the shop. But, still, it is free food, isn't it?

It is another day and I am at the counter, recording customers' items. One loaf of bread, a bag of potatoes, a hot pie, fresh vegetables and apples – five things, written down. A mum with two kids approaches the counter: A bag of potatoes, a hot dog, two hot pies, two sandwiches, a family-sized cake, three apples, two brownish bananas and some lettuce. The retailers have been generous today, sending many veggies and fruits – the lettuce leaves are not so bright green and the texture is slightly wilted, but they are still edible! Customers are reminded that some food is past its sell-by date and that they should use their discretion when consuming it (see Figure 2.7b). A bag of potatoes should be counted as one item; adding another would make a total of ten items for one customer. Do not forget to say 'good night'.

Figure 2.7: Notices displayed in the Free Food Store

The kids are already eating their pies. As they leave the shop, I find myself asking: where do they live in this cold, wet weather?

"Oh, hi, how are you tonight?" I say as another customer, an older man, approaches the counter. "Do you want a plastic bag for your food?" He asks where I am from. Apparently, I am not a Kiwi and not from here! "Turkey", I say. He tells me that his granddad fought against the Turks at Gallipoli. What should I say to this? "Really?" I murmur unintentionally. I am not ready for such a conversation. I do not question what his granddad was doing thousands of kilometres away from his own land. Perhaps I should tell him how colonialism and imperialism make nations enemies of each other while the poor die at the war fronts. I remember there is a saying that your geography is your destiny. Neither this old man nor I can escape our destinies at this small shop, though we are much more than just Turkish or

Kiwi. The uneasiness emerges again and I ask myself: What am I doing here? What does being in Aotearoa New Zealand as a Turkish academic trying to problematize food poverty mean? Does aiming to do critical work have its own identity politics? Would things be different if I were from Aotearoa New Zealand, a Pākehā or a Māori, or perhaps a researcher from the UK? I do not know.

The day ends. Time to calculate the total amount of people who have come to the shop and the total amount of food delivered. One-ledger accounting is simple and easy – it lets the shop be accountable to all through the recorded amounts. The customers and the delivered food turn into numbers that are shared daily with the local community on Facebook, along with aphorisms from famous people. The figures let trustees know about the beneficiaries of the shop, and Mary will use them as a basis to generate funds through numerous grant applications to secure the shop's future. The yearly statistics will show that numbers have increased over time. Counts of nameless customers and surplus food (to some extent counted arbitrarily) become evidence of food poverty in 'the land of plenty'. As the final recording is done after customers leave, the food that is left is taken by other community organizations for another round of circulation – perhaps as stock feed for the pigs. Is the pig still hungry and chasing kids around? The legend continues.

Answers, solutions, imaginations

What do I really do here? Boxing the mildly rotten potatoes, sorting the shelves of bread, cleaning the fridge, collecting food from retailers, community gardens and cafes around the place, arranging the yoghurts and dips inside the refrigerator, talking to other volunteers and John, the manager, asking Mary lots of questions, interacting with the customers, acting as a gatekeeper and guardian of surplus food. Perhaps this is a process of discovery regarding what is missed or neglected in our daily lives – as my interviews with the food retailers indicate, it traces back to the story of the bread produced with the fixed ratio of 7 per cent surplus, meaning that after making crumbs out of white bread, the rest (150,000 loaves) become stock feed weekly (in comparison, the Free Food Store gets 750–1,000 loaves per week). It's not surprising that the pigs get huge, eh? Perhaps, I have solid ground for questioning the rationality of the retailers donating food – are they avoiding costs or doing good for society? (I remember the person in charge of coordinating the surplus food at a major food retailer got angry with me when I asked about the costs and told me that of course they care for the community.) In fact, for the retailers and cafes, the costs of the food they donate is covered by what they charge their own customers. There are other externalized costs of production too ('follow the value', as a wise man called Marx may have said more than a century ago). Well-established disciplinary regimes mean the customers of the free shop are not 'consumers' as we know them – those who pay for and buy what they want (though is this freedom?) Hey, Foucault's spirit – are you still interested in critical studies of management, identities and subjectivity?

How do I join the dots while I search for alternatives? Isn't that what the academics on the other side of the bridge do – explain life through theories or try to make sense of the emerging reality by gathering empirical material? In the case of the Free Food Store, I am not sure whether I am observing a success story of social entrepreneurship, with the motivation of creating 'social good', or perhaps another round of market solutions, this time mobilizing the community in the form of a charity shop (Poppendieck, 1998) – a 'win-win' solution (to use irritating business jargon) – without engaging deeply with the broader issues (the corporate social responsibility they promote in fancy business schools, right?). What if this initiative is yet another Band-Aid solution to addressing the needs of the community, driven by both Christian and neoliberal ethics? As individualized 'free market' players, we come up with our own solutions, such as through 'unconditional love'. And, yes, we perhaps love capitalism too. It brings surplus food to us. And there are even those who would argue that being homeless has always been a 'choice' we make in the freest of free markets!

Can the initiative of the Free Food Store be considered food activism, then? Considering the amount of food 'saved', yes, of course; but how about those people who continue to live in poverty? This shop becomes the point of intersection for all these messy and complex questions. It helps me see through what is happening at the heart of this city and in our society against the context of the usual problems of the capitalist world – growth ideology, consumerism, overproduction, inequality, surplus food, food waste and poverty. All in one shop – social complexity at its best! More than that, can I also see the shop as an alternative postcapitalist organizational form? Could it form a basis from which to challenge mainstream production and exchange relations (Gibson-Graham, 2006)? Or am I just being naive?

As I engage with various theories in the coming chapters, I keep wondering whether I am really different. Can I help the community with my presence at the shop and through the study I am conducting? Indeed, what am I to Mary, to the volunteers and the customers? A curious academic providing free labour; just a volunteer; someone who is not Kiwi; a lecturer coming from the other side of the bridge; the threatening academic gaze; a gatekeeper for the food? Is my activist-self welcome here? While the messy complexity of the world is before me, what am I supposed to do with the academy and my academic-self 'from the other side of the bridge' observing the world from a safe distance? Sure, I can go on publishing about what I find and how I make sense of the case from a theoretical point of view. But, my activist-self wonders about reimagining an activist academy based on action and practising differently (Prichard and Alakavuklar, 2019)? Would the community be interested in this idea of an activist academy?

Perhaps, I should begin with the redefinition of *homo academicus* and their practice – research, teaching and service. Isn't this what 'academics' do – start with a definition? I am not arguing that redefinition is easy, considering the destructive impact of the neoliberal university (which is obviously not monolithic but ceaselessly individualizes us and our profession). Some may think I am in a safe and secure position to argue about that (working in a permanent position in a developed country), especially given the rising precarization and casualization of higher education. Fair enough. With all this in mind, why not push the limits more? What I suggest here is related to the political and moral responsibility of doing critical research, since, at least for me, it is all about pointing out inequalities and unfair practices and suggesting viable alternatives (despite the challenges and hardships involved). Then, reimagining an activist academy, or at least working towards it (Contu, 2018), would mean creating a new political and democratic relationship so that theory can be mobilized for social change with real political impact (Rhodes et al, 2018).

I may have crossed the bridge this time. Yet, taking one step further, working towards the activist academy, why not burn the bridge after I move my body and intellect to the other side and do research with the communities, for the communities, and, in a way, coproduce knowledge? I am not the first to argue for this (Chesters, 2012; Cox, 2015; Reedy and King, 2019), but here I suggest a radical departure from 'business as usual' and invite you, my dear reader, to think about reimagining and recreating the academy as well. Here is my invitation: Instead of being tucked into our offices, trying to feed the 'never enough' publishing machine, let's go outside our offices. Let's mobilize ourselves and colleagues, build a collegial atmosphere instead of a competitive one, and initiate dialogue, conversation and debate for change. Let's engage with those communities who may be organized at the margins and trying to deal with ongoing social issues, and let's do our best to contribute to their causes, and if possible radicalize and politicize to address broader issues. Is all of this an easy task? Of course it isn't – but why not? It would mean challenging ourselves, as I described earlier (What am I doing here? What am I to the community?). However, while we may have opportunities to learn from the communities we work with in different ways, our presence brings, to some extent, a challenge for those communities as well, as we create a tiny disturbance through asking some simple questions, use our presence as a question mark, create the opportunity to reconsider how things are organized, try to formulate a complex combination of theory and practice even though we do not know how it will pan out, and ask people to engage in a process of co-learning and coproduction. With this comes the risk of rejection, the challenge of being inaccessible, the inevitable confrontation of power differences. Nevertheless, I can work towards an activist academy by embracing and unfolding such tensions.

Hence, I dream of an academy that is more about learning from common challenges and messy complexities and, if possible, involves experimenting with community organizations to intervene in change dynamics through material, symbolic and political relations in society. Reimagining an activist academy will not only change relationships within the academy and between academics and communities, but also challenge knowledge production as we know it. Why not consider publications as best practices shared with scholarly communities through journals? Why not organize activities that would enrich the shared experience with communities? Why not practise 'scholarship' differently? Why not change the means and ends as we reimagine the activist academy, hoping and working towards acceptance as we cross the bridge?

Referring back to a recurring theme in this chapter, the issue here may or may not be about me, or whether I am different. Here, 'me' is just a case, similar to many other academics, challenged by communities and big societal issues. Yet, with these challenges comes an opportunity to think, write and act differently. Hence, the tension between the academy and activism may have been resolved through writing and acting differently. My activist-self is trying to drag my academic-self to cross the bridge, to work towards an activist academy for new opportunities, challenges and tensions. More importantly, all these questions and answers, reflections and actions, turn into an invitation to reimagine ourselves, our profession, and create an activist academy in response to the grim realities of our world.

It is believed that the admonishment 'let no one ignorant of geometry enter' was engraved at the door of Plato's Academy. Coming today, with reference to the wise and bearded man I mentioned earlier – who was a fantastic scholar but an activist at the same time, and has transformed our thinking since the 19th century – perhaps the activist academy should have the following engraved on its door (and let no one enter who is ignorant of its challenge): Philosophers have hitherto only interpreted the world in various ways. The point, however, is to change it.

3

Genesis: How Would Jesus Redistribute Bread?

I would like to begin this chapter with an excerpt from a conversation I had with Mary, the founder/director of the Free Food Store.

Founder: So I came back and was volunteering for a couple of organizations, one of which did a community meal a couple of times a week, and they got bread from the supermarket that was left over and gave it to people at the end of the meal.

Ozan: So it was leftover bread or leftover food?

Founder: Well, it was bread in this particular case. That is where it started. I got permission to take the food and put it in the back of my car, and we went ... I drove around the city, knocking on doors and giving out bread. That grew to include other food on top of the bread, but primarily it was the bread that I was able to take, and that was the start.

Ozan: You mentioned you were knocking on doors and you knew the people that were kind of in need of this bread?

Founder: Well, no [laughs]. For me, it was a bit of a faith thing. I would pray and ask God where to send me, and I would literally drive or He would say go to this area, and I would see a house maybe or [somewhere] that looked like ... maybe it didn't have curtains, or maybe I saw some kids ... and so I would just stop, or [rely on an] impression in my spirit [about] where I should just stop. So it was quite random. And there were other times that people had asked me, when it became more regular, when people would try to contact me, ask me if they needed food or knew someone that needed me. So it was a combination of things. But it really was that I drove around and looked and knocked on people's doors and asked, 'Would you like some bread?' Some people said no. Most people said yes. … Most of all, people said yes, but often they would kinda look at me and say, 'What's the catch?', you know … 'Why are you giving me free bread – what do you want?' And I would say [that] I don't want anything, there is no catch, it's just free food, it's free for you. I told them where I got it, and they were really happy to get more food. I guess that really began the journey of dealing with free food, leftover free food.

Before founding the free shop, Mary was already involved in various communities of the Christian faith. Through her faith-related network, the Free Food Store came into being. The initial documentation and business plans for the Free Food Store show that the Christian faith has a significant role in Mary's life and the shop. For instance, in the statement of belief in their business plan for 2013–2015, the Free Food Store board of trustees state 'that a Christian worldview is the way to positive change and the redemption and betterment of society'. They also state that 'through the Free Food Store, we are able to serve the community in accordance with Christ's teaching and our Christian Ethic. People so assisted become enabled to reach out and touch others in their community, through stories of love and support they have received in their own lives.'

The altruistic attitude and positive view of human nature and social relations are evident throughout the Free Food Store's own narratives. This is reflected in the use of the terms 'unconditional love' and 'unconditional giving', through which the faith aspect becomes visible and tangible in the daily life of the shop. Notices with these phrases hang here and there in the shop as reminders of the shop's stance of religious tolerance towards people in need: people are welcome regardless of who they are – poor or wealthy, Pākehā or Māori, student or employee, unemployed or employed. The use of these terms is also an attempt to provide a dignified encounter, unlike the experience of going to food banks. Without contextual knowledge, these references to unconditionality might be considered a form of platitude. However, the more time I spent at the Free Food Store, the more I felt the aura and impact of faith. Christian faith is always there as a guiding philosophy, like a compass.

For instance, many of the volunteers are connected with different religious communities and churches. Given the small scale of the city where the shop is based, it is common for networks of religious organizations to work closely together. I went with Mary to an event where multiple faith-based organizations, such as The Salvation Army, had organized a free dinner for various groups in need. Mary tells me that co-organized events such as this take place regularly, and the Free Food Store provides surplus bread. These invisible networks and relations also facilitate recruitment of volunteers.

Many volunteers join the Free Food Store through word of mouth via these networks and church connections. The shop manager, John, is also a believer and joined the Free Food Store first as a volunteer, before taking up the responsibility of coordinating volunteer shifts and managing day-to-day operations.

As Free Food Store documents show, guided by the Christian philosophy and ethics, and framed with a charity logic, the Free Food Store offers a service to the community, helping people who are in need. In doing so, the shop is also connected with a broader network of faith-based organizations that mobilize to co-organize events, like the dinners, and to do advocacy for the disadvantaged groups of the society. The promotional materials posted on the notice board in the shop demonstrate its (in)formal links with similar community organizations in the city and region.

While filling out the volunteer form, I noticed that there was a box to be checked to indicate that the applicant has been informed that the Free Food Store is a Christian organization. I had found this strange, since this religious aspect had up to this point not been clear to me. I had only been aware of the narrative that *everyone* is welcome. During my induction as a volunteer and on other occasions, rather than stressing the faith element, Mary emphasized that the free shop is a place for everyone as long as they respect others:

'We have a Christian ethos, which are the driving values, but I would not describe it as a Christian organization. We are not trying to convert; we exist to love, feed and to help. ... In terms of not having to pay, we are very much about the people of the community.'

I presumed that this emphasis was made since I am from Turkey (where the population is predominantly Muslim); however, I do not practise religion at all. This is an interesting point for me, since my aim is to be an insider understand what is going on in the Free Food Store. However, my limited religious knowledge may mean I am unaware of, or perhaps less exposed to, any religious discourses and symbols there. In other words, my 'secular' eyes may have missed some details as I engaged with the Free Food Store. At the same time, as I am neither Christian nor part of any religious networks, I may have better positioned as an observer to pick up on and address faith-based practices.

Aside from the notices about 'unconditionality' and the materials on the board, the most visible religious practice is the prayer just after 'grab time' for volunteers (the ten minutes before the shop opens its doors to customers; see Chapter 1). This is a fixed ritual each day the shop was open to customers, coordinated and attended by Mary.

Once the volunteers grab some food to consume immediately or take home in the evening, and the amount of food is noted for the day, we all gather closer to the counter (... Mary's office is located next to it), and Mary tells [us] what is happening around ... the shop. This is a moment for a quick daily chat with the volunteers or a news-sharing opportunity, about the Free Food Store. After this sharing moment finishes, volunteers stand in silence and Mary prays and thanks God. Then, she goes outside with a loudspeaker to inform the customers about the daily availability of the food. (Field notes, 5 February 2015)

Some volunteers are also explicit about the role of faith both in their own lives and at the Free Food Store. For them, volunteering at the shop is a way of expressing and practising their religion.

'The Bible says if you love me, feed my sheep. And I feed them if they are hungry and come to me. But He also says physical grievance isn't everything, and there is spiritual food, and I don't feed that. We used to, but we don't do it anymore. But my Christian view is my own personal view, not that of [the Free Food Store]. But before, we had Bibles on the shelf for people to take, but they appear to be taken off, and that's the way it goes.' (Oliver – Volunteer)

'But I still come back to the base of meeting a need. Being a Christian, it relates to my worldview of how it's better to give than not to if you have the means.' (Sarah – Volunteer)

Like Mary, John also emphasizes the limited visibility of religion at the Free Food Store and distinguishes it from other faith-based organizations:

John: Mary and I have had this discussion about how religion shouldn't be pushed or explicit. I wouldn't want to hang around if there were posters about turning to Jesus in the store or if we were encouraged to speak to people about Christianity.

Ozan: Why's that?

John: It's just annoying. People shouldn't have to go through that to get free food.

Ozan: But on the other hand, it's still there? That feeling?

John: Yeah, she says a prayer. People have asked me if I'm a Christian since I work at the store.

Ozan: Who – the customers?

John: Yes. I guess because they probably know Mary is a Christian.

Ozan: So they know about the praying?

John: [They] probably don't ... I don't know if this is wrong or right, but you have a lot of charities like The Salvation Army and St Vinny's that have strong Christian roots and do social services. So they see another practice, and I guess it's an assumption.

Ozan: So it's an implicit part of the Free Food Store? What are your thoughts on that?

John: Well ... I don't feel it ... maybe the only time is when there's a prayer. It's interesting when Mary is away – I don't say one, but instead I ask if anyone would like to do one. But people often want me to do one, as I guess it's just a nice thing.

Ozan: That's interesting.

John: Yeah, there was one they asked me to do, so I did, but I felt like it was something they appreciated for some reason [laughs]. I don't know why they'd appreciate it. It's just a moment of quiet where we ask if we can have a good night.

It should also be noted that the majority of the volunteers I interact with are not religious. Some state explicitly that they volunteer simply to do good for the community. This also aligns with Mary's perspective that they are not there to convert people but to rescue food. This means that it is mainly the driving ethos and goals of the organization that are religious, reflected in some practices and motivations of Mary, John and some volunteers. Yet, unlike other faith-based organizations, faith or religiosity is not deliberately reproduced through day-to-day activities (Salonen, 2016). Faith-based ethics of care for the community, altruism and unconditionality are embedded into the symbolic cultural layer of the Free Food Store. No specific Christian denomination is promoted, nor are the volunteers only from one particular church. Unlike many faith-based food charity organizations that are directly supported by churches and explicitly practice religious doctrine (see also Power et al, 2017), the Free Food Store is broadly influenced by the Christian faith aspect but driven predominantly by helping people in need – everyone is welcome. As noted in Chapter 1, this is reflected in the profile of customers and volunteers. Religious tolerance is mobilized to offer a dignified experience for the customers to come and pick what they want while considering others' needs. They do not need to prove or confess how poor or disadvantaged they are (see Chapter 5 for more on this).

Given the long history of faith-based organizations and their expression of religious ethics through provision of social services and engagement with social and economic issues, what the Free Food Store does may not be novel. Related to this historical mission, charity as an organizational form has long been a means to assist people in need, though this has been highly criticized. Given the complex relations bringing the Free Food Store to life, how should we make sense of the charity form and its relation to faith? Can we approach religion as a generative resource to think about alternative organizations? Of course, these questions become difficult in the face of the consequences of the neoliberal experiment in the Aotearoa New Zealand context.

At this point, I want to open a parenthesis about my framing of neoliberalism, since it has become a field of study in itself, with multiple and contested approaches (Cahill et al, 2018) to this 'still-moving target' (Peck, 2018, p xxiii). Despite its wide-ranging and even contradictory use in different disciplines, there are central tenets of neoliberalism as an economic, political and social project (Springer et al, 2016) that impose market efficiencies over social relations through deregulation and privatization, mobilize the state as the overseer and promoter of (free) market relations, and view the (responsible) individual as human capital to be invested and developed (Brown, 2015; Fleming, 2017). Ultimately, as a set of regulatory policies adapted differently concerning context-specific variables (Jessop, 2018), it serves for capital accumulation at global level (Harvey, 2007).

Aotearoa New Zealand was rapidly introduced to neoliberal policies by the fourth Labour government in the 1980s, and this transformation of the economy continued through public policies under different governments throughout the 1990s (Kelsey, 1995). Beginning with deregulating financial and commodity markets, state-owned enterprises were either privatized or corporatized,[1] and governed through the new public management paradigm. Public policies on subsidies (for example, in farming) and welfare were reconfigured dramatically, and state provision was reduced. Employment law changed, privileging employers and negatively impacting unionization (Redden et al, 2020). These continuous reforms were presented as apolitical and for the good of society. However, former Prime Minister Jacinda Ardern has acknowledged that these were a failure (see Cooke, 2017). As a result of these economic policies, inequality and poverty have increased and so has the demand for food banks (Watson, 2019).

Closing the parenthesis and referring back to the question, posed in the previous chapter, of why the Free Food Store is organized as it is? If it is faith, how does that serve to mediate relations and mobilize people and resources to save surplus food and redistribute it?

---

[1]   While privatization means changing ownership of a state-owned asset to a private owner, corporatization refers to transforming a state-owned asset into a corporate structure. Once a publicly owned asset is corporatized, privatization becomes easier.

Between the moral and the political

To begin with, we should set out the paradoxical situation the Free Food Store finds itself in. On the one hand, they do charity work, give out free food and, very likely, build a paternalist relationship, maintaining an imbalanced power relationship with their beneficiaries (see Chapter 5). On the other hand, let me remind you that since their beneficiaries are hard to categorize, the organization's initial applications to become a registered charity, and therefore be able to collect donations, had been refused. Additionally, their mission emphasizes rescuing food and helping people, goals directly related to environmental and social sustainability practices. According to the shop's website, from its beginning in 2011 up to September 2023, more than 557,000 people have received food from them, and the shop has removed more than 8.878 million food items from the waste stream, which (if we apply an average of 350 grams per item) is more than 2,781 tonnes (metric) of food. In addition to being part of religious networks, they are connected with organizations against food waste and other free food shops, sharing best practices and creating awareness about food waste and using surplus food differently.

Following Dey and Humphries (2015), the Free Food Store should be contextualized in terms of the tension between the moral and the political – doing charity work and limiting the politicization of food poverty while tackling social, economic and environmental issues, within their capacities, and empowering communities. With this argument, I do not intend to see an ideal or pure organizational form that would solve all complex societal problems at community level. In conversation with the literature on food banks, charities and social action by community-based organizations, I want to argue about the limitations and the potential of such organizations. In doing this, I also want to demonstrate how macro structures (for example, religion, economy) relate to the Free Food Store and its practices.

Regarding the limitations of the moral motive, we see criticisms about food banks and their function in developed countries. For instance, Poppendieck (1998) argues that food banks are responses to dramatic shifts in socioeconomic regimes, similar to those that have taken place in Aotearoa New Zealand (Kelsey, 1995). As neoliberal regimes have been implemented, through prioritizing market solutions and limiting state assistance, unemployment has risen and the safety nets established by the welfare state mechanisms have deteriorated. In this context, the response of 'giving' and 'donating' have established a positive sense of doing good for society, promoting charity logic. Regarding the apolitical motive of the Free Food Store, it would be unfair not to acknowledge their positive impact on the environment and communities. But let me delve into the charity logic that is central to such organizations.

So, what is wrong with charity logic?

When the problem is framed as a 'hunger' issue, it sounds reasonable to 'feed people in need' with 'surplus food' while also 'doing good for the community'. However, others posit that the issue is more structural and political than that. We find answers from Riches (2018), who argues that food poverty is a complex problem that needs broader questioning of neoliberal capitalism and corporate practices. While various phases of neoliberal policies have led to rising unemployment, economic inequality, precarious working conditions and low wages (Humpage, 2014), it has become difficult for families to sustain themselves, one result being food poverty.

Meanwhile, the corporations have a better hand as they control food systems, can negotiate lower wages and are able to donate tax-deductible surplus food to food banks and food charities. Hence, food charity emerges through and is reinforced by the perception of 'good corporate and individual citizenship' (Salonen, 2018, p 4), which is well aligned with neoliberal ideology. Within this set of relationships, food banks turn food surplus and excess into a resource and utility of last resort assistance. The notions of surplus and excess can be questioned, as they demonstrate that there is enough food but it is not distributed fairly. Hence, food poverty, similar to the shortcomings of housing and other essentials, becomes a signifier of structural inequalities and begs for structural solutions (Salonen, 2018).

Riches (2018) calls for a structural inquiry that asks why charities emerge and why we need them, taking a political framing as opposed to the simplistic perspective that focuses on 'people in need and hunger'. In other words, he seeks to draw attention to the mechanisms that continuously reproduce food insecurity and waste and reminds us of the importance of the right to food. As Riches argues: 'It is about the universal right of vulnerable individuals and families to be able to feed themselves with choice and human dignity. It presses the case for rethinking what we mean by solidarity with the poor and why the human right to adequate food matters to us all' (2018, p 2).

Caraher and Furey (2018) also point out the mechanisms of depoliticization and establishing the social legitimacy of food charity. They argue, for instance, that the official engagement of religious charities with the public authorities to coordinate food assistance

> allowed the development of systems based on 'voluntariness' and the appearance of delivery by religious organisations, all of which is contrary to public welfare and does not spring from any legal responsibilities of the food providers or legal rights of the food recipients. As with other countries, as public service budgets are squeezed, charities step into the breach to deliver short-term help; of course, this shorter term has no end for many. (Caraher and Furey, 2018, p 27)

According to Caraher and Furey (2018), the nature of food as a necessity and the convenience of delivering food (instead of funds) directly to people facilitated the taking over of food welfare struggles by charities, as a moral response. Meanwhile, the fact of abundance of food keeps this charity logic going. Salonen addresses how the process by which faith-based food charity organizations play a critical 'middleman' role leads to 'rescaling and decriminalising excess and tuning the vice of waste into a virtue' (2018, p 4). Out of this virtue and altruism, based on the redistribution of surplus food to fight food poverty, more questions emerge concerning feelings of shame, loss of dignity and increased inequality (Caplan, 2017; Caraher and Furey, 2017). Hence, food charity has become a sector in which the neoliberal state leaves it up to voluntary initiatives to provide a solution.

Faith and food poverty

While food charity may be presented as a moral and altruistic solution to a socioeconomic problem, its roots can be found in faith and religion. Sharing food, dealing with hunger and helping those in need are central to the Christian faith and others, and these teachings mobilize communities.

For instance, there are many verses in the Bible encouraging the giving of food:

Isaiah 58:10: If you pour yourself out for the hungry and satisfy the desire of the afflicted, then shall your light rise in the darkness and your gloom be as the noonday.

James 2:14–17: What good is it, my brothers and sisters, if someone claims to have faith but has no deeds? Can such faith save them? Suppose a brother or a sister is without clothes and daily food. If one of you says to them, 'Go in peace; keep warm and well fed,' but does nothing about their physical needs, what good is it? In the same way, faith by itself, if it is not accompanied by action, is dead.

Proverbs 22:9: Whoever is generous will be blessed, for he shares his food with the poor.

While giving food and supporting the poor is encouraged, the story of Matthew 26 and the reference to the poor (11) should be recalled:

Jesus Anointed at Bethany
    [6] While Jesus was in Bethany in the home of Simon the Leper, [7] a woman came to him with an alabaster jar of very expensive perfume, which she poured on his head as he was reclining at the table.

[8] When the disciples saw this, they were indignant. 'Why this waste?' they asked. [9] 'This perfume could have been sold at a high price and the money given to the poor.'

[10] Aware of this, Jesus said to them, 'Why are you bothering this woman? She has done a beautiful thing to me. [11] The poor you will always have with you, but you will not always have me. [12] When she poured this perfume on my body, she did it to prepare me for burial. [13] Truly I tell you, wherever this gospel is preached throughout the world, what she has done will also be told, in memory of her.'

The message in this verse is interesting because it not only assumes that Christians will always be there to help the poor but also suggests they will address inequalities and poverty. This is a point I will come back to later.

From another religious perspective, Islam encourages its believers to practice Zakat (to give one fortieth of one's wealth as charity as an obligation annually) and Zakat al-Fitr (specific form of charity given at the end of Ramadan mostly in the form of fixed amount of food) to support people who are poor and in need. It is also believed that the prophet of Islam said:

Oh people, exchange greetings of peace, feed people, and you will enter Jannah [paradise] in peace.

Free the captives, feed the hungry and pay a visit to the sick.

He is not a believer whose stomach is filled while his neighbour goes hungry.

Therefore, religious organizations worldwide are involved in food charity and assistance programmes, providing shared meals, soup kitchens and food banks. As a result, food charity and social support by churches or religious institutions have been with us for a very long time. The critical question is how it became so widespread and a preferred problem-solving mechanism in affluent societies such as Aotearoa New Zealand (Lambie-Mumford and Dowler, 2014). In her detailed account of the development of food banks in Aotearoa New Zealand, Watson (2019) argues that churches have traditionally been involved in coordinating food banks. Yet, with the structural economic reforms leading to neoliberalizaton in Aotearoa New Zealand, in line with Riches' observation, food charity and similar food assistance programmes emerged as preferred institutional solutions. It is also striking to note that more and more people report no religion in Aotearoa New Zealand's official statistics. While in 2001 just over 1 million people reported that they had no affiliation with any religion, in 2018 this number rose to more than 2.2 million (Stats NZ, 2019). Hence, while religious affiliation is losing ground, faith-based charity solutions continue to fill the void left by the established, but limited, welfare mechanisms in terms of meeting people's needs.

Making sense of faith and organizing

While the modernist narrative has seemingly pushed religion from public life into a more private sphere, as Gümüsay argues: 'Effectively, the world as a whole has either never really dis-enchanted, or it has been re-enchanted. Religion is a significant source – and thereby explanatory variable – of beliefs, values, and meaning. Our theories need to reflect this empirical reality' (2020, p 859). Historically, given the modernist roots of the discipline of management and organization (Reed, 2006), it evolved as a secular field, and faith as a matter of subject in itself did not find much space despite its relevance in organizational life (Tracey et al, 2014; Gümüsay, 2020). Regarding the epistemological-ontological positions analyzing the role of religion and spirituality in organizations and organizing, Peltonen (2017) identifies three approaches:

- *the rational-scientific approach* – this considers religion and spirituality as a set of variables to be measured and modelled by the objective (positivist) scientist;
- *the cultural-social approach* – this sees religion and spirituality as a source of meaning to understand and interpret social and organizational relations by closely observing related beliefs and practices;
- *the metaphysical-theological approach* – this identifies religion and spirituality as an answer to the most fundamental questions, and is studied through participating and reflecting by a theologically informed practitioner.

In social science, while the modernist tradition considers faith a conservative force that should be made obsolete, the Marxist tradition approaches religion as an ideology derivative of a particular material reading of societies (Escobar, 1997). Hence, it is not surprising that Marx saw religion as the 'heart of the heartless world, and the soul of the soulless conditions. It is the opium of the people' and the people's response to grim living conditions (1844, para 4). However, from a different perspective, faith can become a 'generative resource' for social transformation (Escobar, 1997, p 82).

Mylek and Nel argue that faith plays a critical role in mobilizing civil society against poverty through its: social networks, facilitating reciprocity and trustworthiness; philosophy and teachings, calling for action to remedy poverty; and cultural power, the 'ability to influence political processes and outcomes by appealing to "cultural resources" – symbols, ideologies, moral authority and cultural meanings – which enable messages to resonate with wide audiences, generating more tangible forms of power' (2010, pp 85–86). They emphasize that combining moral concerns with social justice resonates with various groups in society in terms of tackling poverty. Conradson (2008) also indicates that faith-based organizations in Aotearoa New Zealand have the capacity to act beyond emergency relief and engage with broader social justice issues concerning inequalities.

Along the same lines, Van Buren et al (2020) argue that religion can be applied analytically as a macro social force. Their pragmatic approach to defining religion as 'broadly, collectively, and in terms of self-reference' is helpful since it does not delve into intra-theological contestations and acknowledges 'the diversity of ways in which religious belief systems are organized' (Van Buren et al, 2020, p 802). In studying the role and impact of religion, they also argue in favour of a descriptive approach, assuming no normative position, to demonstrate how such a macro social force leads to the emergence of organizational mobilizations and acknowledges the role of practices. As key institutions, faith and religion have always mediated social and organizational relations. The crusaders, colonialism, liberation theology and many other movements are either directly driven by religious motives or at least have vital components of faith in them. In line with these theoretical viewpoints, I adopt a descriptive approach emphasizing cultural and social aspects. I recognize the significance of beliefs and practices and their influence on how organizations operate.

Mediation of faith in the Free Food Store

Concerning this relationship between faith, religion and organizing, the Free Food Store makes the impact of this macro social force visible through day-to-day practices, as faith mediates a particular form of organizing in the neoliberal context in Aotearoa New Zealand. Following Mylek and Nel (2010), it is fair to argue that as a part of the broader loosely connected religious social network, the Free Food Store is driven by faith-based philosophy and teachings, subtly shaping its narratives and practices. Mobilizing moral/cultural assumptions to tackle food waste while helping those in need has also been evident since its inception. Such organizing is informed by Christian beliefs and practices that promote being good, just and moral, and acting according to altruism. In particular, practices of unconditionality play a key role, meaning the Free Food Store has the characteristics of charity. As discussed in the following chapter, this mediation of faith creates various meanings and a sense of belonging for the founder, the manager and some of the volunteers.

Unconditional love and unconditional giving are distinguishing characteristics of the Free Food Store. Unlike the traditional food bank, which asks for evidence of limited income (that is, means-testing), the

Free Food Store attempts to avoid the stigma around 'being in need'. The purpose is to help people with dignity. The volunteers, residents and political figures of the city welcome this approach. They all praise this policy of no judgment and being open and accessible to all.

Riley (Volunteer):	[It] takes in surplus food from around the community and hands it out quite freely. I'd say it's quite admirable and is good too … when they set it up, they saw an opportunity and went for it, so it's quite entrepreneurial.
Ozan:	So, what do you think about the idea of giving food for free?
Riley:	I love it. I mean, I'm a boring old communist [laughs], but I think everyone should have necessities of life freely, so I think it's great there's a chance to do that in a capitalist society.

Unconditional giving and lack of financial reciprocity were the characteristics that drew me into the Free Food Store and led me to view it as a compelling case of alternative organization – how can a shop be free and create an environment in which customers can choose what they want (which is different from the way food banks work) with no monetary exchange?

Nevertheless, the more time I spend at the Free Food Store, the more I see that some of the practices lead to a negative perception of the customers – the people in need. For instance, the queue that tends to form around an hour before opening time at the Free Food Store means that customers are visible to the city as they waited for food. Crucially, the perception of people in the queue that is held by the community and the owners of other shops in the neighbourhood is different from the perception held by those at the Free Food Store. For instance, in an informal conversation with the owners of a shop across from the Free Food Store, he explicitly expresses his dislike of the Free Food Store and recounts the usual misperceptions, loaded with prejudice, about customers – alleging they are lazy people who spend their benefit payments on drugs and alcohol, and are dependent on the Free Food Store for food rather than working to pay for it. Hearing such narratives, which represent and reproduce the neoliberal ethos about 'individual success' and 'poverty as an individual problem', is unsurprising to me. Similar criticisms emerge from more established charity organizations that are in favour of "identifying those who are in need and acting upon it" (informal conversation with Mary) so that they can prevent dependency on community solutions like the Free Food Store and encourage people to improve their skills and find jobs.

There are various responses from the community members to these criticisms. Some argue that people who criticize the customers do not know how difficult it is to get welfare from governing bodies. They state that even though some individuals misuse their money, it is a fact that many people who are in need cannot easily access the welfare mechanism and so many families may need extra support. Some others acknowledge that the shop's beneficiaries are primarily from very disadvantaged backgrounds, and believe that such criticisms are utterly unfair.

> 'In a way, the Free Food Store does exploit the system [pauses]. It doesn't encourage people to go out and get jobs and have money to buy their own food. It creates dependency, and it's a handout; we don't really provide people with means of supporting themselves. But then there are mentally ill people who aren't able to sustain themselves; in a way, because the benefits system has failed so many people, this free food offers an option out. In terms of society, I don't know if it's hugely beneficial [pauses]; it's difficult to say.' (Sarah – Volunteer)

While some volunteers admit that there might be dependency issues, they think such problems have to be accepted as part of human nature. As Mary puts it, better that the food goes to people in need rather than landfills. If this is the case, and given the criticisms, how can we frame the role of the Free Food Store as a charity with good intentions in a neoliberal society?

Faith as the surrender or mobilizer: where to look for alternatives?

While there is moral reasoning to support faith-driven charity work, it comes with the risk of depoliticization of the problem and investing more at an institutional level in a paradoxical system that reproduces the problem of food poverty (Humphries and Dey, 2015). Those working for charities are also aware of the political shortcomings of this kind of system. While my conversations with the volunteers and with Mary address the political root cause of the problem as structural overproduction due to market needs and consumerism, given the scale of the problem the solution is mainly handled through a moral language around unconditionally helping those in need, with dignity. This is in line with Watson's (2019) findings on food banks and food rescue organizations in Aotearoa New Zealand. She argues that the political edge of these initiatives has gradually been lost and that the void has been filled with moral and environmental justifications against the backdrop of neoliberal policies.

While the positive side of such initiatives is well observed in terms of meeting people's needs, financially empowering and creating leeway, welcoming people from all walks of life, promoting sustainability and reducing food waste, there remains a challenging amalgamation of faith, neoliberal individualism and depoliticization of food poverty. Therefore, it can be argued that the neoliberal discourse hampers the critical and political edge of faith-based organizing to promote social justice. Meanwhile, its *moral* narrative is praised through 'responsibilized communities'. Gauthier et al argue that

> neoliberalism goes a step further by redefining the social sphere as a form of economic field. Thus the economic field comes to include and subsumes all forms of social life and human action. The transformation is complete: from being embedded within the social, the political and the religious, the neoliberal age is that in which market economics are henceforth that in which other social realities are said to be themselves embedded. (2013, p 13)

Peck and Tickell argue how such community initiatives can be seen as 'the mobilisation of the "little platoons" in the shape of (local) voluntary and faith-based associations in the service of neoliberal goals' (2002, p 390). Hence, in line with the assumptions of the neoliberal ideology concerning the role of the Free Food Store, points can be made regarding: the voluntarism of the responsible individuals triggered by concerns of morality, faith, social justice and ecological sustainability to deal with a societal problem; the reliance on market actors (big retailers, local cafes) for solving societal issues; and the assessment of poverty as an individual failure (or even a choice) while acknowledging the difficulties of living with it. These aspects play a critical role in transforming political edge into moral narrative so that the issue (for example, food poverty) can still be governed. Symbolized by the saying 'we do what we can do', in the face of structural and overwhelming issues of food surplus, food waste and food poverty, society reinforces and welcomes the morality of the cause. Hence, the political potential of faith-based mobilization is neutralized through a moral language affirmed by a self-governing community that is sustainably tackling the issue of food waste.

Recalling the message of Matthew 26:11 is key at this point. Despite the multiplicity of interpretations and practices concerning food poverty (Allen, 2016), given the dominant function of food banks and charity solutions, one can argue that Christianity is built on the assumption that poverty will always be part of society. Hence, inherently, mobilization should be about helping the poor, not transforming the structural relations reproducing poverty. Then, despite the potential to engage with social justice issues, the question is: should we expect much from this kind of moral mobilization? Since its genesis, faith may not have had the political tools to take on the structural relations that got us to the disparity and inequality people experience today.

Nevertheless, arguing that these organizations are the forebears of neoliberal ideology and practices would be unfair. As Lindenbaum posits, and as the diversity of personal views in such initiatives tells us, community organizations 'do not play a prominent role in governing client behaviour, do not create private property rights, and most importantly, do not price food at the market rate; food banks neither advance neoliberal discourses nor produce neoliberal subjectivities' (2015, p 382). On similar lines, Williams et al (2012) point out the contingent nature of neoliberalization that has been a product of multiple assemblages, opening up the possibilities of contestation and co-constitution. Following their reasoning, 'we, therefore, need to be critically hesitant before prematurely labelling discourses of welfare dependency, responsibility, and empowerment as intrinsically "neoliberal", and we might instead analyze the disparate streams of rationality that produce fundamentally different landscapes of political intelligibility and possibility in different social milieux' (Williams et al, 2012, p 1486).

Concerning the dilemma of the political and the moral, my point is more about acknowledging the potentialities of the moral cause than accepting the limitations of depoliticization. While such an approach may sound romantic, I would argue otherwise and begin working with the processual and co-constitutional nature of the relationship between faith, neoliberalization and organizing. Despite the claims concerning the limitations of a neoliberal charity logic, there might be emerging possibilities for transforming the same logic, again, thanks to the mobilization of faith for social justice, from a moral point of view. Like the economic sphere (Gibson-Graham, 1996), faith is not a monolithic structure, despite the fundamentalist impositions, and the diversity of different faith-based practices should be noted and welcomed.

In the case of the Free Food Store, this is seen at local level through the unconditional solidarity of the community to care for each other and support their well-being, as well as having concern for environmental sustainability. Even though faith has played a critical role since the Free Food Store's inception, the organizational practices are not evangelical and aiming to create a monolithic community of its own. As evidenced by the profile of community members, the Free Food Store is open to diversity and difference. Hence, alternative beliefs, practices and subjectivities are already present, however tangled with the socioeconomic complexities (Lindenbaum, 2015).

While arguing the surrender of faith to neoliberal ideology may offer its own insights, there is a risk of misrepresenting or missing the potentialities of initiatives like the Free Food Store. Perhaps this is the nature of alternative organizations, operating mainly in a grey area and enriching our imaginaries further to think 'outside the box'. Breaking down the monolithic understandings of neoliberalism and faith is critical to understanding the value of 'alternatives' while acknowledging their tensions, challenges and possibilities (see Chapter 7). As argued by Williams et al, 'faith both enacts neoliberal formations and embodies resistance to them, and it will be tracing these practices and moments of enactment and subversion that will lead to a more nuanced understanding of the faith-based-organization phenomenon in the contemporary city' (2012, p 1494). Therefore, it is a matter of future questioning and organizing whether faith-driven moral claims can turn into, or return to, political struggles, which may not be the priority of the members of the Free Food Store but perhaps are for social scientists like me.

Would you agree, my dear reader?

4

There's No Such Thing as a Free Lunch, But …

> **Vignette: What an abundance of loaves of bread!**
>
> I drive the van into a vast complex from which various foods are being distributed throughout the region. I have to be extremely careful, since large trucks are coming and going. I park, put on the reflector jacket and open up the van. The bread packed in trays is ready to be taken, labelled Free Food Store. These loaves of bread have been returned to the distributor in various qualities and varieties. What an abundance! I count at least 120 loaves of bread; hundreds come from other retailers daily too. It is stunning to see the total amount of bread, which would go to waste or become stock feed if the Free Food Store did not exist.

Once I collect the loaves of bread, they immediately belong to the Free Food Store to be (re)distributed during the day. This non-monetary exchange reminds me of the saying 'there's no such thing as a free lunch' and triggers my interest and imagination about whether we could organize our economy based on 'free giving'. My dear reader, have you ever been in a shop that gives things away for free, with no monetary exchange? It's not that common, I would assume. Hence, bear with me, as I would like to introduce you to some terms of critical political economy – yes, you are right, Marx's spirit is still with us in this chapter, though I make some challenges to his assumptions.

I wonder: as commodities and their market values dominate our economic practices and imaginaries, what happens when food is not sold and becomes a non-commodity, as in the case of the food that goes to the Free Food Store? Advancing the question further, what would our organizing be like if there were only 'use value' of the things we need? Having analyzed the mediation of faith as a part of the symbolic layer in the previous chapter, here I focus on the material/economic layer of the Free Food Store and reveal how the use value of surplus food and labour of community members mediate (non)capitalist value relations.

Before I delve into the diverse (non)capitalist economic practices of the Free Food Store, let me tell you about the flow of food that is moving on from the commodity form (that is, any good/service that is sold in the capitalist market that has exchange value). The Free Food Store collects surplus food which is no longer a commodity and can be considered excess or waste by producers and retailers. However, the food is still edible and has its use value, primarily for meeting people's needs. This is where the Free Food Store plays a critical intermediary role by bringing together the food and the people. Therefore, surplus food, with its use value, becomes the source for and driver of organizing, and the volunteer labour is interwoven around it to let the free shop function. Different from the exchange value of commodities, I argue, the use value of food and labour mediates social relations. This entails relating people, practices and attributed meanings in a specific setting. How, then, are alternative noncapitalist value relations organized around use value in a nonprofit community organization, and how do they function to sustain the community within and beyond capitalist practices while interacting with them? I follow a different structure in this chapter, beginning with a theoretical discussion to make sense of the economic layer and how value relations are constituted. Are you ready for a theoretical challenge?

Organizing differently

The assumptions about the for-profit managerial firm as the primary economic and social value-generating organizational model and capitalism as the preferred macroeconomic model have a hegemonic position in management and organization studies (Reedy and Learmonth, 2009; Chen and Chen, 2021; Janssens and Zanoni, 2021). As a derivative of this hegemony, capitalist value relations associated with the production of commodities/services and monetary exchange within the commodity-based market economy have been a major focus for scholars of management and organization theory (Jensen, 2002; Lepak et al, 2007; Pitelis, 2009). This hegemonic epistemological and ontological framing not only narrows down other possibilities of organizing the economy, but also neglects the importance of noncapitalist value relations that help communities sustain themselves without the logic of capital (Healy, 2009; Parker et al, 2014a).

In response to this hegemonic framing, there is a growing literature on alternative organizations (Parker et al, 2014b; Schiller-Merkens, 2022). This literature can be categorized according to alterity of values and principles in organizing (Parker et al, 2014a), democratic political governance relations (King and Land, 2018) and their combination with different forms of ownership and profit distribution models (Cheney et al, 2014; Chen and Chen, 2021; Kociatkiewicz et al, 2021). While such studies document the diversity of alternative organizations within the cracks and gaps of capitalist relations (Parker et al, 2014b), there are also attempts to position and categorize alternative organizations within the broader social relations (Parker and Parker, 2017; Zanoni, 2020; Just et al, 2021) based on whether they align with, oppose or substitute for a market economy (Jonas, 2013). However, we lack a theoretical opening to study alternative organizations in relation to the entangled economic practices. Alternative organizations are not isolated islands within the larger economy, as they are inevitably and inherently related to diverse capitalist and noncapitalist practices, accommodating contradictions and tensions (Zanoni et al, 2017; Del Fa and Vasquez, 2020; Vidaillet and Bousalham, 2020). To shed light on the relationality of alternative organizations and untangle the complexity of noncapitalist organizing within and beyond capitalist relations, this chapter brings a 'critical political economy' perspective that focuses on value relations (Prichard and Mir, 2010).

Here, value is taken as a relational economic concept that fundamentally differs from signifying the ethical and political concepts (for example, values, beliefs, principles); however, the two types of concept are interrelated. While value as an economic relationship mediates our exchange and social relations in a given context, our values, beliefs and principles as a set of ethical frameworks guide us, as subjects, within these social relations (Harvie and Milburn, 2010). Value, then, becomes the material analytical entry point for unravelling the complexity of alternative organizing in which values play a role in accommodating religious beliefs, constructing identities and meaning-making. Here, I would like to bring a refreshing perspective to help us think differently about value, value relations and organizing in a diverse economies setting.

The Free Food Store presents a challenging case for addressing the relationality of alternative organizing, since it operates through capitalist and noncapitalist economic practices. The shop primarily relies on the surplus food coming out of capitalist production relations, has minimal wage relations, hosts non-market practices – such as the use of non-commodified (volunteer) labour, non-monetary exchange relations – and creates a community through giving free food. At the same time, like food banks, it is part of a complex and contradictory economic system (Caraher and Furey, 2018). While it rescues food waste and meets people's needs, it paradoxically relies on and supports the same system that normalizes food poverty and Band-Aid charity solutions (Dey and Humphries, 2015; Watson, 2019, p 81). However, community initiatives like the Free Food Store are also capable of 'socially useful production and doing' (Chatterton and Pusey, 2020, pp 41–42) by diverging '(intentionally or not) from private accumulation of monetary value, market competition, and the commodification of essentials and life itself' (Schmid, 2021). Hence, how are noncapitalist value relations organized in a nonprofit community organization, and how do they function to sustain the community within and beyond capitalist relations?

Here, I engage with three strands of literature: alternative organizations (Jonas, 2013; Parker et al, 2014a), value relations and organizing from a critical political economy perspective (Prichard, 2016; Pitts, 2021) and the diverse economies framework (Gibson-Graham, 1996; Gibson-Graham and Dombroski, 2020). While the diverse economies framework helps me highlight the interaction and coexistence of capitalist and noncapitalist practices without prioritizing one over the other (Healy, 2009), value relations offer a theoretical intervention. This intervention can help untangle the complex relationality of alternative organizing. By following the journey of food methodologically (Appadurai, 1988; Marcus, 1995), I demonstrate how alternative value relations emerge at the Free Food Store within a 'highly varied and dynamic ecology of economic practice in which elements interact and combine to produce the outcomes we see in the world' (Peredo and McLean, 2020, p 818). My approach brings forth the mediation of use value – 'the usefulness of a thing' (Marx, 1990, p 126) in satisfying needs and wants – constituting alternative economic, symbolic and political relations against the background of contested socioeconomic tensions embedded in a diverse economic context (Gibson-Graham, 2006; Mirosa et al, 2016). My analysis indicates how capitalist relations enable a noncapitalist parasitic alternative organizational form.

This chapter introduces 'value relations' as a critical political economy framework. I argue that the material basis of organizational relations can be explained through the concept of 'use value' and its mediation. Understanding the relationality of alterity within broader social relations makes it possible to uncover the complex web of interrelationships between capitalist and noncapitalist practices, cultural values and material practices, and food poverty and abundance. By examining the constituted economic, symbolic and political relations, value relations offer a conceptual language to analytically study and untangle the contested nature of alternative organizing within and beyond capitalist relations.

Alternative organizations within and beyond capitalist relations

The literature on alternative organizations sheds light on values and principles (Parker et al, 2014a), democratic practices (Sutherland et al, 2014; Reedy et al, 2016; Daskalaki et al, 2019) and collective, indigenous and common ownership models (Peredo and Chrisman, 2006; Atzeni, 2012; Fournier, 2013; Cheney et al, 2014; Mika et al, 2019; Kociatkiewicz et al, 2021). While these characteristics contribute to inspirational experiments in organizing cultural values, political practices and profit distribution differently, locating 'alternative-ness' within and beyond the prevailing capitalist practices is still an ongoing theoretical puzzle (Parker et al, 2014a; Del Fa and Vasquez, 2020; Vidaillet and Bousalham, 2020). Therefore, there is a growing interest in theorizing alternative organizations according to their relationality with key actors in society (Barin-Cruz et al, 2017), their transformative potential of dominant institutions (Zanoni, 2020; Just et al, 2021) and their processes and struggles to depart from the status quo of capitalist relations (Dahlman et al, 2022).

Jonas (2013) also argues that our theoretical abstractions about alternatives should be based on a relational conceptualization, taking account of their evolving processes instead of fixing them in opposition to the mainstream/ capitalist. Given the diverse, contingent and context-dependent characteristics of alternative organizations, their 'properties arise relationally out from interactions with other (e.g. mainstream capitalist and state) processes, relations and territories' (Jonas, 2013, pp 28–29). Based on this relationality, there are three types of alternative organizations: alternative additional, oppositional alternative and alternative substitute (see Jonas, 2013, p 34).

Alternative additional organizations are aligned with capitalist principles that rely on market practices and exchange relations and offer choices alongside mainstream organizations (for example, credit unions). While they operate within commodity market relations, these organizations may prioritize alternative principles such as autonomy and responsibility (Parker et al, 2014a), alternative ownership models and profit distribution schemes such as cooperative organizing (Cheney et al, 2014). Organizational scholars analyze the tensions between these (progressive) characteristics and the pressures of market relations (Pansera and Rizzi, 2020; Mondon-Navazo et al, 2022).

Oppositional alternative organizations lean towards radical practices, seek autonomy from the state and follow non-market practices to challenge the mainstream (an example is time banks). Social solidarity clinics (Kokkinidis and Checci, 2023), commons-based organizing (Fournier, 2013) and prefigurative community organizations (Schiller-Merkens, 2022) can be counted as examples from the alternative organizing literature. Scholars mainly focus on the transformative potential of (radical) economic practices, the expansion of alternatives to capitalist relations and the emerging organizational challenges.

Alternative-substitute organizations are considered a last resort and a coping mechanism for meeting needs at the local level. At the same time, they may not need to be an alternative to the dominant (economic) practices. They rely on sharing or gift economies, have cooperative labour relations and host alternative value relations, as in the cases of intentional communal organizations (Pitzer et al, 2014) and community kitchens (Willat, 2018). As explained later in the chapter, the Free Food Store can be considered a perfect example of an alternative-substitute organization.

Building on the notion of relationality, I argue for a critical political economy perspective that goes beyond the simplistic dichotomy of capitalist/ mainstream versus noncapitalist/alternative (Chen and Chen, 2021). By focusing on 'exchange relations and questions of value', this approach focuses on the matcrial economic side of (alternative) organizing as a source of explanation, critique and transformation within broader social relations (Prichard and Mir, 2010, p 511). Therefore, critical political economy provides a framework to comprehend the interplay between noncapitalist and capitalist economic practices and how these practices shape and structure our organizational relations on a material level. Through a range of examples, scholars have explored how new possibilities for labour, property and social relations emerge in alternative organizations. For instance, Watson's (2020) analysis of a community-supported agriculture cooperative reveals how such spaces decoupled from the dominant capitalist logic can mitigate the experience of work alienation. Peredo and McLean (2020) highlight the potential of common property-based organizations, such as community land trusts and worker cooperatives, to decommodify land and labour and support livelihoods. Drawing on open-source communities and creative urban scenes, Arvidsson (2009) suggests that positive affective bonds and friendship (philia) can be sources of value that sustain these communities and mediate social relations rather than the dominant market logic and competition.

My analysis follows this tradition of critical political economy that locates organizing within broader social relations and tensions. Specifically, I introduce the mediation of use value in the context of an alternative-substitute organization, which provides a theoretical framework for revealing the coexisting and interacting relations between capitalist and noncapitalist practices.

Use value and value relations as a theoretical intervention within the multiplicity of economic practices

In a commodity-based economy dominated by for-profit managerial firms, value is a relation established through the labour we put in to produce a commodity others will use to satisfy their social needs (Pitts, 2021). This creates an immaterial and invisible relationship that is often hidden during the production process (Harvey, 2014, p 26). Commodities have two forms of value: use value and exchange value. Use value refers to the usefulness of the commodity and how it satisfies our needs. For example, a house can serve multiple functions and can have various qualitative values, such as being a shelter or a place of social reproduction. Exchange value, on the other hand, emerges when commodities are exchanged in the market. This is the moment when commodities are validated and given value through each other. As an example, two kilograms of apples might be equivalent to two metres of linen, which we exchange for their respective use values. The possibility of such an exchange relies on the condition that both commodities have the same value but in a different form (neither apples nor linen). Regardless of the form of the commodities, they have an exchange value expressed in another form, such as price (Marx, 1990, p 127). As a result, exchange value has a quantitative uniformity, represented by money as the universal equivalent to facilitate the exchange of commodities in the market (Pitts, 2021, p 40).

The imperative of capital accumulation has led to a commodity-based economy that values everything in terms of its exchange value (that is, price) in the market, often neglecting other values and value relations that may be essential (Harvey, 2014; Peredo and McLean, 2020). This mediation of exchange value leads to particular capitalist value relations that shape how we produce, consume and live, influencing our understanding of life and our own subjectivities. For example, by selling our labour as a commodity in the labour market, we become part of the production relations and produce surplus value through our labour – the additional economic value beyond the required subsistence to reproduce the labour that the owners of the means of production appropriate. Our subjectivity as labourers, consumers and stakeholders is defined in relation to our participation in economic practices driven by capital accumulation.

However, the economy cannot be reduced to capitalist practices alone, which Gibson-Graham (2006) calls 'capital-o-centrism'. This discourse relegates noncapitalist economic processes to the margins, obscuring their importance and potential to offer alternative ways of organizing economic life. To move beyond this framework, Gibson-Graham (2020) advocate 'reading for difference', which reveals the coexistence of a multitude of economic practices and the complex interrelationships between capitalist and noncapitalist practices (Peredo and McLean, 2020). Noncapitalist practices, such as household relations, raising children, non-commodified labour, cooperative organizing and gift-giving, already exist alongside capitalist practices to meet the diverse needs of communities. These practices sustain life by attending to material, social, cultural, spiritual and emotional needs (McKinnon, 2020, p 116). However, this coexistence is not without tensions and contradictions. For example, domestic labour, a noncapitalist practice, is often intertwined with capitalist practices and can contribute to capitalist accumulation. As a result, the line between capitalist and noncapitalist relations is not clear-cut, and their interactions are entangled.

The entanglement of economic practices also includes multiple noncapitalist economic formations that prioritize use value and mediate social relations, such as bartering, gift-giving and donating (Humphrey and Hugh-Jones, 1992; Rehn, 2014). These formations facilitate alternative value and exchange relations, giving rise to different rules, practices, relations, meanings and subjectivities (Arvidsson, 2009; Prichard, 2016). For example, in the case of gift-giving, the giver may not seem to gain anything materially, but there are associated economic, symbolic and political relations that maintain reciprocity and harmony within the mutual relationship (Mauss, 1990; Graeber, 2001). These relations can also have broader social implications and contribute to the well-being of society as a whole. In this case, an alternative motive, giving, is emphasized as a source of wealth (Malinowski, 2002) that serves social functions, such as demonstrating prestige, status or power, in an alternative social and economic setting (Appadurai, 1988).

Within the entanglement of economic practices, diverse labour and exchange relations can be harnessed to meet community needs. For example, volunteering can be a non-commodified form of labour that is compensated in various ways, including cash exchanges, material goods, meals, appreciation, pride or a sense of self-worth (McKinnon, 2020, p 121). Engaging with diverse economic practices using our labour can result in the emergence and transformation of various economic subject positions, such as waged worker, unpaid family caregiver and volunteer, which have the potential to empower communities to (re)configure social and political relations (Gibson-Graham, 2006; Healy et al, 2020). Thus, with an alternative set of assumptions and economic practices (Gibson-Graham, 1996), use value has a performative impact, creating different meanings and value relations for those involved (Marcus, 1995).

The relations mediated by use value signify diverse meanings for different individuals and can be categorized accordingly. They may take the form of economic relations, involving the material gain, exchange and redistribution of resources; symbolic relations, which relate to cultural, moral and normative positions, such as values, principles and assumptions; or political relations, which pertain to power dynamics and the (in)capacity of actors (Appadurai, 1988; Levy et al, 2016). Examining these value relations makes the entanglement of capitalist and noncapitalist economic practices visible.

The Free Food Store as an alternative-substitute organization is an interesting case for analyzing the relationality of alternative organizations through value relations. In this way, it becomes possible to uncover what makes the Free Food Store and what kind of (alternative) relations, practices and meanings emerge while still being dependent on and located amid capitalist relations. So, how are noncapitalist value relations organized in a nonprofit community organization, and how do they function to sustain the community within and beyond capitalist relations?

From the perspective of surplus food

While the global food system focuses on short-term profits over the qualitative characteristics and use value of food (Elmes, 2018, pp 1054–1055), it is critical to recall the central role food plays as part of subsistence for communities, which helps better address the role of use value in mediating relations, compared to other modes of exchange. Hence, food not only plays an essential role in creating meanings and social formations, but also becomes a critical entry point for analyzing and understanding the organized world driven by capitalist relations (Pina e Cunha et al, 2008). The significance of use value is pivotal in my analysis, as the empirical reality observed within organizational practices and discussions at the Free Food Store revolve not around food prices, monetary transactions, profit calculations, accumulation or competition – concepts associated with exchange value, which facilitates the exchange of commodities; in contrast, the organization's focus rests on surplus food, fulfilling needs, aiding the community and 'doing good'. These aspects are related to the non-commodified facets of exchange relationships and 'socially useful practices' (Eskelinen, 2020). This material and discursive alterity manifested empirically through day-to-day practices and narratives prompted me to consider the alternative economic relationships that make such organizing feasible. Consequently, use value emerges as the theoretical and analytical basis, serving as the focal point for making sense of the Free Food Store empirically.

The journey of food takes place throughout the day, beginning with the collection of surplus food and continuing as it travels to the shop, is reorganized by volunteers and, finally, is taken by the customers and community organizations (see Figure 4.1).

Economic relations at the intersection of capitalist and noncapitalist practices

Given the scale of food surplus, the amount the Free Food Store rescues is tiny. One of the leading distributors donating bread explains that it is common for the bread industry to produce a surplus of 7 per cent. Considering the product range of the food retailers, even a 2 per cent surplus or wastage would mean a significant cost for them. Some businesses need to pay to eliminate food waste, but they do not approach donating surplus food simply in economic terms. Therefore, donating food to the Free Food Store seems like a win–win solution for businesses, allowing them to cheaply eliminate food products that have lost their market value. Social responsibility and business perspective align

Figure 4.1: Noncapitalist value relations through the journey of surplus food at the Free Food Store

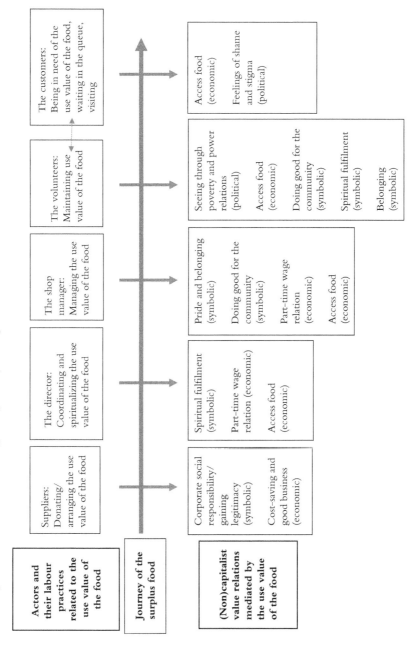

well in this relationship, though with the risk of using charity and unpaid labour for corporate welfare (Poppendieck, 1998; Tarasuk and Eakin, 2005). I asked two representatives from suppliers to the Free Food Store whether they prioritize the cost aspect or the responsibility aspect. They answered:

'Absolutely, it is a fifty-fifty. We want to help the community, and we are much more active now, as the company is trying to do far more in the community than we ever did before. But definitely, it's good business sense, and it's good being a responsible corporate citizen.' (Supplier 3a – store manager of a national retail company)

'So, yes, we save some costs, and other costs are incurred from this programme [referring to the national food donation programme]. For us, it's about doing the right thing, and we're also sending it to people who can eat it instead of going to the landfill. So it's better for the environment, and our CO_2 emissions levels are basically capped at where they were in 2006, and part of that is because we are not sending stuff to landfills to decompose.' (Supplier 3b – head of corporate affairs of a national retail company)

For others, donations are more about doing good for the community with no expectations of financial return (they are paid if they sell the surplus bread to farmers as stock feed). In this case, the surplus food still has an economic exchange value (that is, another form of surplus value) generated by the global/local food system that could be used for capital accumulation if sold as stock feed (O'Brien, 2012). However, it departs from the usual market circulation and becomes a use value. Hence, the Free Food Store becomes a converter of surplus value[1] (excess food production) into use value for the community. Mary, the founder/director, puts this well, saying they are "very much operating ... now within the (economic) system, ... sucking the surplus from the system", which suggests a parasitic but mutually beneficial relationship as the dominant capitalist practices continuously feed into noncapitalist practices in this specific case, with a return in different forms. Therefore, there is a grey area where capitalist and noncapitalist practices coexist and facilitate the functioning of the Free Food Store: capitalist

---

[1] While surplus value refers to the economic value produced by labour on top of the required subsistence for labour power and appropriated by the capitalist class, it also makes sense in this context since it is the value produced in commodity form through the (global/local) food chain that cannot be consumed in the consumption circle. However, its economic surplus value is already appropriated in various forms through its capitalist supply chain. Hence, unless it is sold as surplus food, this surplus value in commodity form turns into use value in this organizational context.

practices inevitably produce surplus food, creating a noncapitalist symbolic value for businesses, which is used as a strategic legitimacy-gaining tool and can potentially turn into monetary value. Although it may not be the primary aim of some companies, it is important to note the indirect economic value of cost-saving and good business practices as aspects of economic relations. The part-time wage relations of Mary, as the director, and John, as the manager, also enable their unpaid part-time noncapitalist labour (that is, their volunteering) and the administration of other noncapitalist practices. Volunteers provide free labour, but their other sources of income and wage relationships should still be considered part of the complex interplay between capitalist and noncapitalist relations in the Free Food Store.

The availability of surplus food as a contribution to the household budget is essential in attracting various groups of people to the Free Food Store. For instance, one volunteer emphasizes how it could be challenging to feed large families (Elaine – Volunteer), while another notes the continuous need to secure sufficient food (Adele – Volunteer). Therefore, the customers as well as the other organizational members (Mary, John and the volunteers) all benefit from the economic convenience of the food. For some, it is also a good deal to exchange non-commodified labour for food, such as during 'grab time' for volunteers (see Chapter 1) or when they feel comfortable coming to the shop as a customer. Therefore, use value mediates the day-to-day economic practices interwoven around food and labour, leading to the emergence of *capitalist* (cost-saving, good business image) and *noncapitalist* (convenience of accessing food without official criteria, meeting needs) *economic relations* at the same time.

Symbolic relations at the intersection of cultural values and material practices

As argued in Chapter 3, faith and religious ethics of care play a critical role in this complex set of relations, which led me to struggle to position myself in this environment.

> It felt quite strange to tick the box in the volunteering form informing me that the Free Food Store is a Christian organization. I wonder to what extent I will be exposed to religious discourses (first day, induction). (Field notes, 27 January 2015)

> The Christianity of the organization is not visible but easily felt. I can say it is in the air. Some volunteers know each other from church communities, but some do not seem religious at all. Nevertheless, we all join in the evening prayer led by the director to thank God for the food to give free and for volunteers (end of the first week). (Field notes, 5 February 2015)

For some organizational members, including Mary, John and a few volunteers (Oliver and Sarah), the use value of food and labour turns into a symbolic resource that satisfies spiritual fulfilment. In response to the ongoing grim economic conditions leading to food poverty, religion is mobilized to be the heart and the soul to comfort people (Marx, 1844, para 4) with a moral intervention. This symbolic noncapitalist value becomes visible through the discourse of 'unconditional love' and 'unconditional giving', to offer a more dignified experience for customers compared to the experience of going to food banks. As Mary puts it:

> 'The food is free for all – giving unconditionally and loving unconditionally. We're wanting to make it available to anyone, and part of that is based on what I didn't know when I started [which] was that [when I was] growing up, my dad was self-employed. And there were times that bills were not paid, and that created hardship in the family and … meant that there was not money for food and other things.'

John's motivation is similar to Mary's, as he is also religious. Working at the Free Food Store helped him get back on track after being unemployed for some years. Nevertheless, managing the use value of the food represents another form of 'noncapitalist symbolic value' for him: doing good for the community and being compensated with pride.

Ozan: What makes you feel proud of it?
John: I think it's what we do, it's very unique – we're not a food bank. It's a hip thing to put waste food to better use. We give it away for free without asking many questions. … It's community helping community, the people who volunteer are people who are in the line themselves if they are not working.

For many volunteers, surplus food with its use value carries a different nonreligious meaning based on creating an opportunity to do something good for the community through offering their non-commodified labour to maintain the Free Food Store. They primarily associate themselves with the organization's mission and acknowledge how it is nonjudgemental, altruistic (Elaine – Volunteer) and open to everyone, referring to the lack of means-testing to access food (Rose – Volunteer).

Overall, use value, as a material construct based on labour and food, mediates the variety of individual cultural beliefs and motivations into noncapitalist symbolic relations, practices and meanings that are shared and lead to the fulfilment of organizational members – spirituality, pride, doing good and caring for the community, and belonging. In other words, cultural assumptions and values as a set of moral guidelines help organizational members find meaning by interacting with the material practice of giving food in response to socioeconomic challenges (Harvie and Milburn, 2010). It should also be noted that businesses have a stake in these symbolic relations, since they can socially valorize their claims about being ethical and sustainable in order to gain legitimacy for their capitalist economic activities.

Political relations at the intersection of food abundance and poverty

Noncapitalist relations in the Free Food Store are not free from their own politics and power relations, which become visible through the mediation of food with its use value against the backdrop of tension between structural poverty and access to food. For instance, some volunteers are explicitly critical of the limits of charity-like structures in the fair redistribution of resources (Riley) and the risks of creating dependency relations (Sarah).

A lot of the volunteers I interviewed know they are in a privileged position and mostly avoid getting food from the shop (in particular, during grab time – something which was also a challenge for me[2]). Yet, for some volunteers, who are also customers on other days, it is common practice to get some food after their morning shifts (before the shop officially opened). However, a class-based difference among the volunteers (and customers) is felt beneath the cooperative labour relations to maintain the Free Food Store. Volunteers are aware of the diverse and primarily disadvantaged profile of the customers, as indicated by one volunteer:

> The majority have mental health issues; many of them spend their days at [social centre]. Some people that come in … for example, several ladies that look very well-dressed, and I'd not be that surprised if they come from work. … We also have a family that comes in with four kids, and she's due any day again, and I remember him saying to the director that they couldn't come in a previous day due to no petrol or something. And they come in pretty much every day, and I think he doesn't work, but then we have two to three people that come in who don't quite need to, and then the rest of the guys are older males

---

[2] Due to limited and changing availability of cold sandwiches and hot pies, I felt like I was stealing food from the customers if I took any of these. I could easily buy a sandwich from a cafe around the corner. However, the more I volunteered at the Free Food Store, the more I believed that I earned a sandwich as a reward for the day's work.

that live on their own and come in for tea really. A lot of young lads but not really a lot of young females. A lot of them aren't necessarily quite poor. (Brigit)

By visiting the shop, customers also have their share of the noncapitalist value relations in political forms. They meet their needs without any formal means-testing; however, there is an implicit stigma around being visible in the queue outside the shop. The queue is one of the major issues discussed at the shop, and during my fieldwork there was no attempt to deal with it. Mary, John and the volunteers, some of whom are occasionally customers, are aware of this problem and take it as an uncomfortable but inevitable part of the daily routine.

Similar to experiences at food banks (Caplan, 2017; Escajedo San-Epifanio et al, 2017; Caraher and Furey, 2018), those who are outside of the 'usual' commodity exchange relations could feel shame and stigma from society. Despite the Free Food Store being open and accessible to all as a case of potential economic empowerment for communities, gaining (food) without giving (money) creates an imbalanced power relation between the shop and its customers, as it leads to the perception of being 'needy'.

I also note tension among the volunteers when approaching the customers. This results from volunteers' implicit ranking of the customers, based on the volunteers' impressions of the customers' potential needs. Some volunteers reveal to me in an informal conversation that they thought customers with 'fancy cars' should not come to the shop for food. However, the primary motivation of saving food and the values of unconditional giving and love weigh in; hence, no one is refused.

Nevertheless, customers may still be exposed to micro-level disciplinary power relations operating at the Free Food Store. They are asked to be considerate of the amount of food they take – there are many reminders to take only what is needed (see Chapter 5 on power relations). While customers are encouraged to show up and access free food, Mary and John are able, based on their own discretion, to speak to customers about their behaviour. I ask what happens if someone annoys the volunteers or other customers. John tells me that if someone demonstrates consistently disruptive behaviour over multiple days, it is common practice to ask them to leave the shop, and he describes how Mary had handled such a case.

While on one side of the relationship, there is unconditional love and giving at the expense of surveillance, on the other, there is unchallenged poverty and individualized shame. Hence, the community initiative may come with the paradox of emancipation and oppression (Tedmanson et al, 2015). These political relations, mediated by use value, shed light on the dark side of alternative value relations (Watson and Ekici, 2020) and make (food) poverty amid abundance much more tangible and visible.

A noncapitalist parasitic alternative organizing within and beyond capitalist relations

While reading for economic difference (Gibson-Graham, 2020) through use value is helpful to identify distinguishing assumptions and practices (see Table 4.1 for comparisons), value relations, as a critical political economic category, help us acknowledge the complexity and tensions of organizing the Free Food Store within and beyond capitalist relations.

My analysis indicates three major discussion points that shed light on the contribution of this chapter.

The first discussion point is the intricate, entangled and contradictory nature of diverse economic practices and conceptualization of alternative organizations within and beyond capitalist relations. I highlight the relationality and interdependency of the Free Food Store within and beyond capitalist relations, surpassing a simplistic binary view of capitalist/noncapitalist distinctions (Chen and Chen, 2021). Therefore, through the analysis of value relations as a theoretical opening, this chapter demonstrates the intricate nature of diverse economic practices enabling the emergence of alternative organizing and offers a nuanced conceptualization of alternative-ness (Parker et al, 2014a). In particular, I argue that 'reading for difference' (Gibson-Graham, 2020) through use value reveals the entanglement of capitalist and noncapitalist practices and the complex relationality of the Free Food Store. The excesses of capitalist food production, the involvement of market actors with multiple interests, the use of volunteer labour thanks to financial security, the limited wage relations to manage the shop, the donation of food and other resources, and the non-commodified exchange relations coexist and are interrelated in this organizational case. This entanglement of diversity is also reflected in the way community members think and act, as in the noncapitalist unconditional giving and loving accompanied by the assessment of people based on the commodities they have.

The second discussion point is the mediation of use value and the constitution of economic, symbolic and political relations in an alternative organization. The use value of surplus food and labour assumes a performative and generative function in mediating the relations between the organizational members and their economic practices, assumptions, meaning-making and subjectivities. This comprehension enables an analytical approach to untangling the economic practices and diverse relations sustaining the Free Food Store. Thus, the intersection of economic practices and diverse relations becomes visible and begins with the donation of surplus food and the exchange of non-commodified labour practices in different forms (that is, spiritualizing, managing and maintaining the use value of food). While the community members have convenient access to

Table 4.1: Capitalist and noncapitalist economic forms and the case of the Free Food Store

	Goods and services become	Mediated by	The form of exchange is based on	Expressed in terms of	Driven by
Capitalist	Commodity	Exchange value	Money	Quantitative: price	Logic of capital: accumulation and growth
Noncapitalist	Non-commodity	Use value	Non-monetary	Qualitative: socially useful doing and production	Well-being of communities
Free Food Store	Surplus food Voluntary labour	Use value of food and labour	Labour vis-à-vis diverse interests and relations	'Religious care' 'Doing good for business' 'Doing good for society' 'Being proud'	Meeting the needs of the community by saving surplus food

free food to meet their needs without any money transaction, businesses not only act responsibly but also valorize such practices in capitalist terms (cost-saving and good business). These material practices also lead to multiple symbolic (non)capitalist relations that show how community members make sense of their involvement at the Free Food Store. While some have spiritual fulfilment due to their religious beliefs, some enjoy belonging and doing good for the community with pride. While the shop is sustained for and by the community with a different set of assumptions and diverse economic practices, it continuously reproduces power relations that discipline the labour of customers – queuing, being visible and feeling stigmatized. As a derivative of the dominant market relations leading to (food) poverty amid abundance, the Free Food Store facilitates a (in)capacity to act within the defined organizational norms. While customers are free to choose, within the limitations of the food that is available, they always need to consider others.

The third discussion point is capitalist economic practices enabling noncapitalist parasitic alternative organizing. The findings reveal a relationality between the coexisting capitalist and noncapitalist practices. In the case of the Free Food Store, capitalist practices enable noncapitalist alternative organizing. This is an interesting finding considering the literature on alternative organizations positioned as initiatives to act against the capitalist establishment with their differences (Del Fa and Vasquez, 2020; Schiller-Merkens, 2022). As this chapter illustrates, without capitalist relations, the noncapitalist alternative nature of the Free Food Store would not be possible. This can be explained by the alternative–substitute nature of the Free Food Store. It neither fully aligns with commodity-based market relations nor contests them, making it an interesting organizational case. Due to its business model, likened to that of food banks, the Free Food Store is part of a complex and contradictory economic ecology (Peredo and McLean, 2020). While it serves communities by empowering them through redistributing surplus food, it relies heavily on the larger economic system, which is driven by exchange value and producing excesses, and is susceptible to inequalities and food poverty simultaneously (Caplan, 2017; Watson, 2019). Yet, interestingly, owing to non-commodified wage, labour and enterprise relations (Gibson-Graham, 2020), acting like a noncapitalist parasite creates something good – a self-governed 'doing' for and by the community, independent of the alienating logic of capital (Chatterton and Pusey, 2020; Watson, 2020).

In other words, the growing surplus value of an economic activity driven by exchange value not consumed through capitalist market relations, combined with the labour of community members, facilitates another economic activity mediated by use value. As a result, capitalist relations enable alternative organizing sustained by and for the community through a dependent, noncapitalist parasitic relationship with the larger economic system. While the exploitation of noncapitalist relations (for example, domestic labour, care work) for capital accumulation is critically analyzed (Hardt and Negri, 2017; Fraser and Jaeggi, 2018), the Free Food Store presents a different dependency relation and coexistent economic relations.

Concluding remarks

Despite the burgeoning literature on alternative organizing, the notion of alternative-ness and its conceptualization in relation to broader social relations are still ambiguous (Parker et al, 2014a). No inherently good or bad alternative organizing forms exist that help us form ultimate judgments (Parker and Parker, 2017). Hence, we need a theoretical opening to understand alternative organizations' complex and interdependent relationships within and beyond capitalist relations (Jonas, 2013; Barin-Cruz et al, 2017; Del Fa and Vasquez, 2020).

Value relations offer a relational perspective and a nuanced conceptualization of alternative organizations to fill this gap. As I argue in this chapter, the entanglement of capitalist and noncapitalist economic practices enables a multiplicity of alternative organizational configurations and pockets of possibilities in which communities can create spaces relatively independent of the logic of capital and capital-o-centric assumptions (Zanoni et al, 2017).

Despite organizational dependencies and limitations amid capitalist relations, we see a miniature of a noncapitalist economic world with its own power relations, organized around use value and socially useful practices (Eskelinen, 2020), which is different from the commodified set of relations seeking ceaseless capital accumulation (Harvey, 2010). All this diversity of noncapitalist practices and value relations occurs due to the enabling of capitalist relations and excesses of surplus, ultimately facilitating an alternative-substitute organization. By rendering such relations visible, the case of the Free Food Store invites organization scholars to think beyond commodity-based economies and for-profit managerial firms and take into account the contradictory and entangled economic relations that can host alternative organizations in different forms.

The critical political economy framework (Prichard and Mir, 2010) helps us theorize alternative (substitute) organizations by acknowledging their material relations and embeddedness in broader contested and contradictory social relations. Taking use value as an entry point presents multiple theoretical openings to explain the alterity of practices, power relations, subjectivities and meanings, and their complex and intertwined relations with other dominant and alternative economic practices.

Therefore, my approach in this chapter extends the alternative organizing literature by introducing use value to analyze the relationality of alternative organizations. It provides a language to conceptualize alternative organizing within and beyond capitalist relations and makes multiple configurations of coexistence apparent. By analyzing the mediation of use value, economic, symbolic and political relations become visible against the backdrop of a complex web of interrelationships. In the case of Free Food Store, this complex coexistence between capitalist and noncapitalist relations materializes as a parasitic relationship that community members sustain. Furthermore, value relations, as a critical political economy framework, critique how power relations are organized structurally around value and exchange relations. Therefore, by untangling the intricate relationship between capitalist and noncapitalist economic practices, this framework provides a holistic understanding of a community organization as an alternative-substitute, presenting not only the 'good' side of noncapitalist performativity of value relations but also the dark side of such complex relations.

This chapter presents an ethnographic case of a small-scale alternative-substitute organization and invites more studies to critique and develop the repertoire of use value in other alternative organizational settings. Future studies on value relations and alternative organizing may focus on new theoretical and empirical questions regarding the performative role of use value at the micro, meso and macro levels, the role of alternative organizations in transforming or reproducing capitalist social relations (see Zanoni, 2020) and the subsumption of noncapitalist alternative relations by capital (see Hardt and Negri, 2017).

5

Take What You Need

Vignette: Limits of unconditional giving and unconditional love

It is a typical Thursday and I am helping customers choose hot food. 'Hot food' could refer to a variety of foods from local food outlets, such as pies, fish and chips, and hot dogs. This is collected from bakeries throughout the day, and from donor cafes at around 4.30 pm. While customers come and go, in a separate room, we prepare the food to be placed in the small heating units, which are sitting on a bench that customers pass as they approach the counter. As I check what was left in the heating units, I hear Mary's voice confronting a customer. From where I stand, I can see the customer with many loaves of bread. She asks him whether he needs that much food. Following Mary's intervention, he leaves some of the loaves back on the aisle. This is the first time the notices were explicitly voiced and practised during my volunteer shifts - 'Take what you need and do not fill your pantry'. Apparently, 'unconditional giving' and 'unconditional love' have limits when it comes to protecting the interests of the common good.

This incident makes me wonder whether the 'Free Food Store' is indeed 'free' enough. It is clear to me that some control mechanisms have been established within the day-to-day organizational practices. Mary, as founder/director, and John, as manager, have legitimacy, based on their roles, to intervene if customers do not stick to the rules and take more than they need. And volunteers are in a position to act as both helpers in and overseers of the practice of free giving.

As described in previous chapters, on a usual evening, one volunteer controls the inflow of customers and has the legitimacy to prioritize families among the customers waiting outside the shop. Once the customers enter, they see two volunteers next to the fridges. These volunteers help customers choose from the dips, yoghurts, desserts and sandwiches. This also applies to the fruit and vegetable section and the hot food section. Occasionally, depending on the food available that day, some negotiation might take place. For instance, when a customer comes to the Free Food Store alone and asks for a large cake from the 'family fridge' (where the larger packages of food are stored), inevitably, they need to present an excuse – their family members are sick at home, could not come to the shop or have to wait in the car. Volunteers do not have the right to question customer motives – they must practise unconditional giving and unconditional love. Yet, they also want to be considerate of the families who come next. These are the moments when I have to embrace the tension of negotiation, when the customer asks for 'one more' sandwich, yoghurt, dip, cupcake or whatever is available. It is difficult if there is limited food that day.

It is unreasonable to think that anyone can get what they want, in a limitless amount, and this expectation is managed through the rule of 'take what you need and do not fill your pantry'. This rule can work in two ways: it can empower the customer to have a dignified experience in relation to not asking for any means-testing and reminding to consider others it can also be used as a control mechanism, since there is no clearly defined ratio of food per person. While the volunteers assist and control the amount of food given out from fridges, or the amounts of fresh produce and hot food that are given out, for bread and other types of food (for example, cans of food, tea, confectionary), the customer decides how much they need and they take the items themselves. The hierarchy of choices also plays a role – hundreds of loaves of bread versus dozens of cold sandwiches and hot food. Cups of yoghurt, litres of milk and sometimes salmon flakes would come into the shop in vast amounts. Daily, the hot food and sandwiches are the first items to run out. Throughout this process of redistributing food, volunteers become, explicitly, the primary gatekeepers of food and, implicitly, actors of surveillance.

How would you feel in this shop, my dear reader? Assume that you are on your way home and feel hungry, and you want to have a sandwich at the Free Food Store. You might get in the queue, converse with the volunteers, grab a sandwich and then make it count. Let's think together, along with some theoretical interventions. Returning to my initial question in this chapter, stretching the meaning of 'free' from 'something you have or use without paying' to 'being not restricted, controlled or limited', I ask: what kind of freedom do we see here? Freedom to come and choose from the available food while being exposed to some disciplinary practices as volunteers and customers? For me, this begs a Foucauldian analysis since, through daily material practices of distributing food and mobilizing discourses around freedom and needs, not only does subjectification emerge, but the shop becomes a kind of panopticon in which the behaviour of organizational members is controlled. The Free Food Store organizes its own 'freedom'.

Freedom

While theories of freedom abound in social science and humanities, Berlin's (1969) conceptualization of 'liberty' has been influential. He argues about positive and negative liberty, in which the former addresses constraint of behaviour, while the latter is concerned about the lack of it and individuals or groups being able to act without any interference. Hence, the individual can take action on the premise of 'freedom from' interventions and interferences, while there can be circumstances facilitating 'freedom to' act. From a different angle, MacCallum (2006) offers an alternative triadic relation to frame freedom, which goes beyond the positive-negative binary and argues about the agent, their purpose and the constraints around the action. Baker reminds us that in a social context, individual freedom has to be curtailed in the interests of freedom for all, as in the example of the state that can 'restrict the exercise of the individual freedom to the extent that this causes harm to others', while absolute freedom may turn into the rule of the strong over the weak (2006, p 206). Arendt (1968) approaches freedom as a matter of action to start something new, emphasizing the burden of sustaining the act of freedom. Hence, it is an ongoing challenge, 'in need of being re-accomplished on an ongoing basis', that renders acts of freedom fragile, uncertain and temporary (Lindebaum et al, 2022, p 1866).

Yet, as Lindebaum et al (2022) also remind us, enjoyment and exercise of freedom are mediated through socioeconomic relations and the context in which we find ourselves. In a society dominated by capitalist relations, from a Marxian perspective, due to alienating social relations, it is impossible to achieve freedom. At the meso level, the organization, the Free Food Store is an alternative substitute organization which is a last resort for communities. From this perspective, in a free market society, there is not much freedom of choice left for those who need the Free Food Store, the people who find it challenging to make ends meet. So the question is, as an alternative charity organization embedded in a challenging socioeconomic structure, can the Free Food Store offer a context in which people can exercise freedom?

Given the essential role of disciplinary practices and surveillance mechanisms for the common good of customers, I go back to Foucault. Foucault's work has been instrumental in analyzing the role of daily practices and discourses in constructing power relations. Hence, power is not centralized in a person or an institution per se; power emerges through practices and interactions as a web of relations (Foucault, 1991). Hence, it is a matter of how day-to-day organizational practices and mechanisms lead to a particular form of power relations enabling/constraining the freedom of subjects involved.

I argue that freedom takes place in the moments of negotiation between customers and organizational actors who have some kind of control over the food. Hence, it is not about volunteers and staff acting in roles; it is the way the shop organizes daily practices and how customers negotiate their needs in the face of discipline and surveillance that shapes and structures the boundary conditions. Therefore, in the end, there is an organized and disciplined freedom.

Although the setup of the free shop may seem intentional, the assistance offered by volunteers and the surveillance that is carried out lead to conditions of unintentional disciplining. This kind of discipline inevitably creates a space to exercise freedom, but in a particular way. In this chapter, I offer a perspective that sees freedom as fragile and uncertain, and that acknowledges action, agency and the differences between positive and negative freedom. It is a dynamic approach to freedom, emphasizing relationality and negotiation against the background of boundary conditions in the Free Food Store (see Lindebaum et al, 2022).

On the one hand, the Free Food Store provides negative freedom for the individual customers, as they are 'free' to choose what they want without any means-testing or proof of identity. This is facilitated by the religious discourse of 'unconditional giving' and 'unconditional love'. On the other hand, this negative freedom is conditioned through boundary conditions for the benefit of the community, since the food is scarce. This scarcity is highlighted by 'take what you need and do not fill your pantry'. Hence, considering the needs of Other customers becomes a disciplinary invitation leading to positive freedom. This is provided in the assistance from volunteers and the surveillance of customers' behaviour inside the shop. The Free Food Store can be taken as a place of positive freedom created through community action to open space to meet the community's needs. In other words, it is a freedom that creates a world that functions for the benefit of the community as a whole (Lindebaum et al, 2022).

Nevertheless, against the background of this tension between negative and positive freedom and the action of the community, disciplined freedom emerges that is negotiated, fragile and breached daily by customers attempting to get more food and perhaps using excuses to do so. While the Free Food Store attempt, in their own way, to regulate behaviour, this is constantly challenged. How can we make sense of this?

Foucault and the dispositive

To explain disciplined freedom at the Free Food Store, I rely on Foucault's work on the notion of dispositive, which brings together disciplinary power, discursive practices and subjectification. Raffnsøe et al argue that

> Foucault articulated a notion of power which showed how subjectivity could be understood as a product of disciplinary mechanisms, surveillance techniques and power-knowledge strategies. Instead of

being perceived as a passive object or mere recipient, human agency could be seen to play an active role within mechanisms of power, permeated as the latter are by self-discipline. (2019, pp 161–162)

A Foucauldian perspective invites scholars to note principles, practices and processes to analyze organizational cases (Knights, 2002; Weiskopf and Loacker, 2006).

Traditionally, Foucault's work is categorized into three domains: discourse and knowledge (archaeological period), power and institutions (genealogical period) and ethics and self-conduct (ethical period). In organization studies, this effect is seen through studies focusing on disciplinary power, politics of discourse, governmentality and subjectification, ethics and care of the self (Raffnsøe et al, 2019). While some commentators argue that this periodization indicates discreet progress of Foucault's theoretical development, the dispositive has recently been introduced as a concept that pulls multiple threads from different periods and ideas together. Hence, the dispositive concept can be considered the 'disregarded intermediary' that constructs the links between different phases of Foucault's work (Raffnsøe et al, 2016, p 274). In conversation with Raffnsøe, Gudmand-Høyer and Thaning (2016), Raffnsøe, Mennicken and Miller (2019) and Villadsen (2021, 2023), I use the dispositive to explain disciplined freedom in the Free Food Store.

The initial translation of Foucault's *le dispositif* from French to English referred to 'apparatus' instead of 'dispositive'. Yet, as argued by Raffnsøe et al (2016), the dispositive provides us with a better grasp of Foucault's meaning through its common English usage – 'something that disposes or inclines' or 'has the quality of disposing or inclining' (Oxford English Dictionary, nd).

Foucault defines the dispositive (translated in the following as apparatus) as

a thoroughly heterogeneous ensemble consisting of discourses, institutions, architectural forms, regulatory decisions, laws, administrative measures, scientific statements, philosophical, moral and philanthropic propositions – in short, the said as much as the unsaid. Such are the elements of the apparatus. The apparatus itself is the system of relations that can be established between these elements. (1980, p 194)

Building on this definition, Raffnsøe et al argue that 'the dispositive is concurrently a grouping of heterogeneous components, tangibles, and intangibles, situated within an arrangement, as well as the transversal set of connections between these components. The dispositive is of a relational nature, rather than of a substantial kind' (2016, p 278). Hence, Villadsen likens the dispositive to an 'ensemble' comprised of procedures, regulations, instruments, institutions and statements that are derivative of a particular strategy connecting them (2021, p 475).

As 'one of the most powerful conceptual tools introduced by Foucault' (Rabinow and Rose, 2003: xv), in this chapter, I use the dispositive as an analytical and methodological tool (Villadsen, 2021) to reveal the interplay between multiple power relations and how this leads to disciplined freedom. Once organizations are considered in relation to the dispositives (that is, constructed by but also part of the dispositives), the limitations of organizational analysis concerning the relatively deterministic dichotomies between structure and agency, freedom and power, continuity and change, material and discourse, inside and outside the organization are left open to multiple possibilities (Raffnsøe et al, 2016, p 274). Therefore, organizations become spaces of multiple dispositives that clash, contradict or complement each other. Organizational subjectivity is constructed and emerges within the intersection of these diverse dispositives and multiple power strategies, and there is always space for individuals to negotiate, manoeuvre and resist (Alakavuklar and Alamgir, 2018; Villadsen, 2021). In particular, through the metaphor of ensemble, the dispositive helps me bring discursive and material practices together to demonstrate how the disciplinary regime is constructed yet navigated and negotiated.

An organizational analysis based on the dispositive(s) sheds light on the complexity, multidimensionality and overdetermined nature of constructed power relations and organizational practices. Overdetermination is a key concept here (traced from Freud to Althusser and from Althusser to Resnick and Wolff) to address how 'things' come to be as a result of the combined effect of multiple causes, as opposed to a mono-cause related to an essentialist reading. Therefore, entities are constituted through a process that takes place against the backdrop of 'pull and push' of diverse effects (Resnick and Wolff, 2013). We need an entry point to theorize these co-constituting relations and processes, and following the Foucauldian tradition, this would mean taking 'relations of power' as an entry point.

The dispositive as a framework acknowledges the multiple sources of conditioning of normativity and the potential of agency engaging with them within the web of power relations that are overdetermined by discourses, practices and institutions. 'Various kinds of pervading, yet not all-powerful, dispositional logics come into play and concur to create a multi-layered field of normativity' (Raffnsøe et al, 2016, p 285). Therefore, the dispositive, as an analytical and methodological tool: opens up possibilities to go beyond dichotomies and acknowledge multiple both-ands instead of either-ors; is against the epochization and periodization of societies (for example, disciplinary versus control versus post-disciplinary or post-control) by recognizing the intertwined nature of multiple 'ensembles'; provides an open-ended analysis that is non-deterministic; and is interactional and relational concerning the role of agency that is not docile, passive or fully disciplined.

From a dispositive perspective, power is directly linked to the exercise and management of freedom through the discursive and nondiscursive elements of the ensemble. Therefore, power is not only relational but also 'pluri-directional', affecting the dispositions of others and our own (Raffnsøe et al 2016, p 287). Accordingly, 'organisations hold neither an ultimate source of power nor a unifying perspective that determines how problems are constructed and solutions identified' (Villadsen, 2021, p 478). Hence, the dispositive becomes performative, dynamic and relational as it renders organizational principles, practices and processes, as well as subjectivities, possible through multiple strategies of power. Therefore, the setup of the dispositive and the relations established around the dispositive can be contested. This set of ensembles presents an open-ended structure while its boundaries are negotiated, contested and reworked (Kokkinidis and Checci, 2021).

While Raffnsøe et al (2016) propose three prototypical dispositives (law; discipline; and biopolitics, security and governmentality) following Foucault's work, based on my observations I offer a dispositive of the Free Food Store centring on the 'free customer', which is the subject constituted by the dispositive. In structuring the dispositive, I get my inspiration from Nazir, who argues that 'the dispositive ... oscillates between different elements and thus emerges for the observer as something that depends on the specific set of relations that renders it visible and thinkable' (2021, p 111). Therefore, the dispositive brings together the multiple elements of materiality and discourses.

The dispositive of the Free Food Store

There are four major elements in the dispositive of the Free Food Store: Neoliberalism, Sustenance, Faith and Community and others. Their interrelationship observed through practices and discourses help me reveal the specific power relations emerging in the shop (see Figure 5.1).

The Free Food Store emerged against the background of challenging social and economic inequalities, which are derivative of the neoliberal experiment in Aotearoa New Zealand (Kelsey, 1995). Like other significant economic policy changes in the Australia, the UK and the US, the welfare state was butchered, public services were introduced to a market mentality, and state-owned enterprises were rapidly transformed into corporations. The state took a coordinator role, allowing market forces to govern social and economic relations; as Humpage (2014) argues, going through the stages of 'roll-back' (1984 to 1999), when welfare state mechanisms were destroyed,

Figure 5.1: The dispositive of the Free Food Store

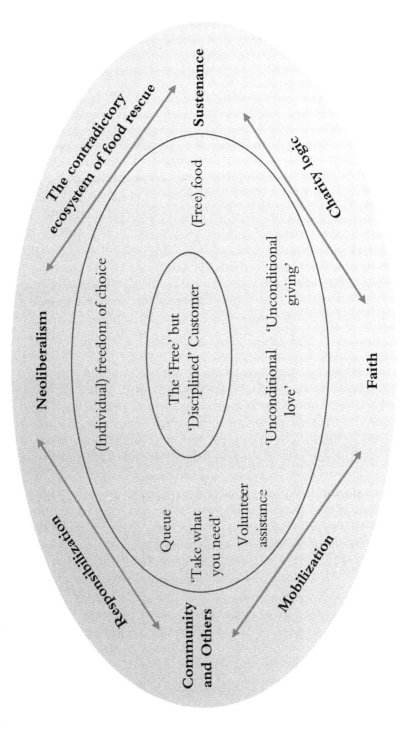

'roll-out' (1999 to 2008), with the WorkFirst approach and positive social rights, and 'roll-over' (2008 to the present), during which time social rights have been retrenched. While the residuals of the welfare state are still in place (for instance, in public health), for a 'better' service, you can have private (health) insurance; (similar to the cases in Ken Loach's 2016 film *I, Daniel Blake*) the welfare support systems are bureaucratized and driven by a 'market ideology', potentially putting people into the 'poverty trap' (Baker and Davis, 2018).[1] In such a context, the disciplinary mechanism of the market operates through the state by categorizing the 'poor' who can 'work' and expecting the 'poor' to 'confess' how 'poor' they are when they need to engage with social welfare mechanisms (Möller, 2021).

As a result of these major shifts in Aotearoa New Zealand, the collective psyche of society was replaced by the competitive individual who is asked to 'choose freely' their future in a free market society. This 'negative freedom' at a societal level is also reflected in the discourse of the Free Food Store and in daily conversations there. For instance, to make the point that the shop is different from food banks that are identified with Christian religious groups and churches, Mary, John and the volunteers often stressed the lack of means-testing and the opportunity the 'customer' has to choose what they want from the food that is available. The use of the term 'customer' can be directly linked to the discourse of neoliberalization, constructing society as a market filled with competitive individuals as a workforce and consumers who ceaselessly turn the wheel of the economy to produce growth. The welfare mechanism, the market and the communities do not refer to 'social citizenship', but the market actors maximize their interests as *homo economicus* (Fleming, 2017). This is well put by van Dyk (2018), who says it is not only individuals who are responsibilized, but also communities, as a part of neoliberalization, to extract value from social reproduction. Following my argument in Chapter 3, I need to reiterate that these relations at the macro and meso levels are not fixed, since they are always in the process of co-constituting each other as part of assemblages (Williams et al, 2012). Therefore, they are always up for contestation by the actors involved.

From a Foucauldian perspective, we see another technology of government (Foucault, 2008) that operates through community solutions informed by neoliberal logic, assessing civil society through the lens of production and exchange relations (for example, the WorkFirst approach). Governmentality scholars point to this kind of responsibilization as a practice of 'government

---

[1] I spent one of my shifts with a volunteer who was part of such welfare programmes. He was not that talkative but he mentioned that he needed to spend a certain amount of time volunteering. Another volunteer talked about the 'workshops' her colleagues had to attend.

at a distance' (Rose, 2001) instead of arguing how charities fill the void left by state retreat (Möller, 2021). It is also argued that such responsibilization applies to those who are already marginalized or disadvantaged (Strong, 2020). In such a context, homelessness, for instance, can be perceived as a 'responsibilized choice' by an 'individual' who is one of the free members of society, as indicated by John in an informal conversation about the profile of the customers at the Free Food Store. This neoliberal logic manifests as freedom of choice in this context.

The other important part of the dispositive is the need for sustenance, which has come under pressure due to shifting economic policies. As argued by Reynolds et al, 'lines of socio-political disadvantage (re)produced in different ways by successive waves of neoliberalization in Aotearoa/New Zealand have promoted the vulnerability of particular groups to suffering food insecurity by reducing their capacity to cope with life's difficulties' (2020, p 148). Yet, they indicate other sociopolitical complexities intensifying the pressure and vulnerability on food security, such as gender and ethnicity in a postcolonial context. As shown in previous chapters, Mary, John and the volunteers acknowledge the impact of lower incomes and financial pressures on households accessing food. While neoliberal logic is connected to sustenance issues, the dispositive demonstrates how the Free Food Store becomes a technology providing access to free food. Furthermore, in line with the previous argument on freedom of choice, the shop not only help people access food with no monetary exchange but also offers choice within limits defined by the shop.

Faith, as an institution, also plays a critical role as a part of the dispositive. Following Chapter 3, the altruistic nature of faith and the religious ethics of care, related to Mary, directly impact organizational behaviour. Concerning food insecurity and poverty, faith is mobilized to comfort and aid people in need (Marx, 1844; para 4); in congruence with the setup of the dispositive, it renders both 'freedom to' choose possible and engage with the transaction through 'freedom from' means-testing and other conditions.

Nevertheless, this individualistic ethos of freedom to choose has boundary conditions due to food scarcity (though it is abundant in principle). Hence, the community and 'the Other' become the disciplinary component of the dispositive. The surveillance mechanism and boundary conditions are set through the discourse of 'take what you need and do not fill your pantry', as well as the queueing and volunteering practices for the benefit of customers. The customer becomes visible due to their needs and carries the risk of stigmatization and feelings of shame before getting into the shop. While the efforts and activities of the Free Food Store are welcomed by many, and volunteering is acknowledged as a contribution to the community, it comes under the 'gaze of society'. Hence, the Other, the community facilitating access to free food, can also become the 'eye' observing and conducting surveillance inside and outside the Free Food Store. While this is a lenient discipline process, as mentioned in the vignette above, it gives legitimacy to the founder and the manager to intervene in the process of 'freedom to choose' as a case of positive freedom benefiting the community.

The contradictory logic of food rescue in the form of charity becomes visible through the dispositive. While neoliberal policies lead to food poverty and insecurity, surplus food becomes available through the functioning of the same economic and political forces (Watson, 2019) to provide sustenance. As argued in Chapter 3, faith and religion play a facilitation role not only by morally intervening in the social and environmental issue at hand through charity logic but also by mobilizing the community that acts as a source of alternative solutions, but with its own disciplining mechanism.

As a result, the Free Food Store becomes one of the components of the ensemble, with its own set of practices and discourses that are the derivatives of the dispositive shaping and structuring the customer, who is free to choose from what is available in the shop in a disciplined manner. Therefore, at a discursive level, the customer is free to come, choose items and engage with the shop by deciding what they need (though it is questionable whether they would have alternatives if the Free Food Store were unavailable). Meanwhile, such freedom comes with the inevitable condition of being 'unfree' to avoid potential stigma and surveillance.

Moments of 'more freedom' through 'disciplined freedom'

Despite the long tradition of focusing on the 'control' side of disciplinary power relations in organization studies, Foucault (1982) acknowledges the role of agency and its potential for resistance and freedom. Accordingly, for Foucault, power and freedom have never been about possession; rather, they are relational constructs that can be exercised through the web of relations. Therefore, where there is power, there is resistance due to its relational character (Foucault, 1978, p 95). While the dispositive leads to the subjectification of the customer as a free but disciplined actor through the gaze of the community and other practices, the subjectification is always contested due to the relational nature of freedom and relations of power. Hence, the customers are neither docile bodies nor the puppets of the discourses (Newton, 1988); they are part of the dispositive as agents that can engage with action and potentially challenge the dispositive. Acknowledging the role of agency, Villadsen argues that the dispositive is 'continually transformed through actions. Instead of a fixed and deterministic structure, the dispositif appears as a moving "battlefield" shaped by perpetual struggle, unfolding through the tactics that individuals pursue in their self-constitutive practice' (2023, p 72). In such a context, 'resistance is not to be conceived as an oppositional reaction, but rather as an already active and transgressive force rendering organisational order feasible and dynamic, but also provisional, precarious, and modifiable' (Raffnsøe et al, 2016, p 289).

While the dispositive of the Free Food Store renders relations of freedom and power visible, it also demonstrates the boundary conditions of the disciplined freedom offered to the customers. To summarize, as a case of negative freedom, the shop provides an alternative 'freedom of choice' with no conditions, as it is possible to feel like a 'customer' in a shop despite there being no monetary exchange. As a case of positive freedom, customers are asked to be considerate of others so that more people can benefit from the free food. Meanwhile, they are subject to surveillance due to the practice of queuing and through volunteer assistance during the 'shopping' experience. It should be noted that the customer may not have many alternatives to the Free Food Store. Compared to food banks, the shop offers a more dignified option, since customers are not required to 'confess' or 'inform' the authorities about income (or poverty) (Strong, 2020; Möller, 2021). It is indeed a free shop that is open to everyone. Hence, an agent acts within the given constraints that enable and limit behaviour (MacCallum, 2006; Lindebaum et al, 2022). But what does the customer do to gain 'more freedom' in this context?

According to Foucault, freedom means practising a particular form of ethics; it is a question of 'how to live' (1984, p 348) within the power/ knowledge grid (Alakavuklar and Alamgir, 2018). Therefore, freedom of the subject emerges through the technologies of the self and self-work within the conditions determined by the dispositive. It is a continuous process of becoming by reflecting on what is given and imposed on the subject and then acting on it. According to Villadsen, the Foucauldian (ethics of) freedom is 'the self's capacity to command the forces that target the self' (2023, p 76). Considering the dispositive of the Free Food Store, the freedom of the customer begins with reflecting on what is available to them and what kind of spaces they can carve out in such a structured context.

Carving out these spaces for freedom takes various forms in the daily interactions of customers at the Free Food Store. These actions include placing bags in the queue before the shop opens, engaging in extended conversations with volunteers, making deliberate choices between different (sandwich) options, negotiating for, say, more cakes or pies, and sometimes taking more food than is needed. These moments represent acts of exercising freedom, likely benefiting not only 'the self' but also the customers' families. These actions can be viewed as enabling individuals to exercise agency and assert their freedom, even within the context of explicit and implicit surveillance and disciplinary mechanisms.

Here, I need to note that my engagement with customers was limited to conversations as part of my 'gatekeeper' role and when assisting them in the shop, and my talks with volunteers who are also customers. When I help customers at the entrance door or next to the fridges, there are moments of greeting but also talks and negotiations about the availability of the food. They would know that if they were late or at the back of the queue, most of the sandwiches or hot food would be gone by the time they got into the shop. Those at the front of the queue would want to know what was available that day. The availability of surplus food that day and the timing of demands and negotiations (right after the shop opened or just before the shop closed) make it easier for the gatekeepers to show discretion.

I did not see any harm in giving one more cupcake or sandwich if there were enough to go round or if it was close to the end of the day. Theorizing such experiences against the background of the dispositive, these are the moments where the volunteers act leniently while the customers also use their agency to go beyond the defined boundary conditions. The vagueness around the notion of 'what you need' becomes a source of negotiation about the imposed rules and leads to a relational and dynamic demand for more food and more 'freedom'.

Following Lindebaum et al (2022) and in conversation with the scholarly works about the dispositive, I argue that the Free Food Store has a particular understanding of freedom, which is relational, dynamic and contested. It not only accommodates negative and positive freedoms (Berlin, 1969) simultaneously, but also constructs a particular subjectification around the customer who benefits from the shop. This constructed subjectivity, as agency, engages with the enabling and limiting conditions that emerge from the dispositive (MacCallum, 2006). Therefore, there is an action in response to and as a part of the dispositive, which is always a 'work in progress'. As Crane et al (2022) suggest, this freedom does not fit into any continuum, offering an essentialist understanding since it is always negotiated within the given boundary conditions drawn by the dispositive. As a result, disciplined freedom is constructed through the ensemble of neoliberal and religious discourses, the need for sustenance and the daily practices ordering and structuring the flow of an ordinary day. Such freedom empowers community members by providing sustenance, reducing financial burden and enabling agency; however, it comes with the risk of being disciplined, kept under surveillance and stigmatized. Similar to the notion of 'hybrid (un)freedom that simultaneously comprises elements of both unfreedom and freedom' against the background of a particular setup of 'prevailing social and economic relations' (Crane et al, 2022, p 1950), the dispositive of the Free Food Store offers intersecting and clashing forms of disciplined freedom for those who benefit from the shop.

Alternative-substitute organization and revealing power relations – for what?

While community initiatives as alternative organizations may have less hierarchical and community-centred practices, they are not independent of their own relations of power. In this chapter, I play with the notion of freedom as my organizational case identifies itself as a free shop. I position it within the broader social relations by engaging with arguments from Chapter 3. Returning to the questions and possibilities discussed in Chapter 2, I analyze how relations of power and freedom are established in an alternative organizational setting.

In doing this, following Möller (2021), I do not intend to critique the Free Food Store and their practices per se. On the contrary, as I argue throughout the book, what they do is inspiring in many aspects: rescuing surplus food that can become waste, creating community spirit, sustainably meeting the community's needs and creating a space for those who cannot make it to the end of the month. Yet, rather than romanticizing such inspiration, it is crucial to analyze all these practices, which do not take place in a vacuum. Hence, I offer a non-essentialist reading through the dispositive to help us understand what kinds of discourses, practices, and institutions are at play to make the Free Food Store and mediate conditions of 'disciplined freedom' in an alternative substitute organization. As argued by Möller, such studies allow us to 'think outside the normality of' food charity and rescue (2021, p 865) and ask critical questions about the conditions creating a particular subject position at the intersection of multiple power/knowledges grids. Therefore, by going beyond binaries and dichotomies, the dispositive can be used not only to position alternative organizations within the broader social relations but also to make the connections between these relations visible. Once their mechanisms and rules become visible, we can begin to reconfigure the same relations and imagine how an alternative setup would be possible (with its revised and restructured apparatus).

Have you begun identifying and deconstructing the dispositives around you, my dear reader?

6

Beyond the Free Food Store: Building Bridges

At this stop of my journey, I want to reflect on my experience as an organizational researcher at the Free Food Store. Based on the lessons learned, I call for more activist research in the neoliberal academy through activist performativity. Therefore, this chapter not only acts as a reminder of my previous arguments and claims but also offers a more comprehensive resolution to the tensions and challenges addressed in Chapter 2 concerning the role of an academic working with and for a community organization. Hence, my dear reader, it begins to join the dots and offer a future perspective, mainly calling my colleagues to action. While it may present an insider's view of scholarship in business schools, I believe it has much relevance to all of you, given the central role of the university in our contemporary society.

I build my argument on the scholarly conversations about postcapitalism (Gibson-Graham, 1996, 2006), alternative organizing (Parker and Parker, 2017; Zanoni et al, 2017; Just et al, 2021), critical performativity (Fleming and Banerjee, 2016; Reedy and King, 2019) and the activist turn in critical management studies (Contu, 2018, 2020; Prichard and Benschop, 2018; Prichard and Alakavuklar, 2019; Alakavuklar, 2020; Grosser, 2021; Weatherall, 2021). As a case of activist performativity, I present the practice of 'bridging', to inspire and invite my colleagues to engage more with alternative/noncapitalist practices.

While this chapter can be considered a personal 'tale of the field', I believe that the challenges and opportunities related to my experience will resonate with many colleagues who feel disengaged and alienated due to the dominant ideological and epistemological assumptions at business schools. These assumptions include corporation as the norm concerning organizational form and neoliberal capitalism as the taken-for-granted economic model; the top-down technocratic view of 'business managers'; the need for competitive and individualistic research practices that reinforce academics' 'playing the game' of publishing; the need to focus on theoretical gap-spotting in research, which is disconnected from real societal challenges; and the practice of instrumental critique without engaging with the relevant societal actors practising social change. In such a context, 'business school academics are not expected to engage in radical work (that is, to ask awkward questions about the current system, to forge progressive alliances and to build theories and practices that have a deep and intimate critical concern with social, economic and epistemic justice)' (Contu, 2020, p 744). I argue instead that engaging with community organizations creates opportunities for academics to perform scholarship differently and get closer to injustices and practices of social change.

To contextualize my fieldwork, for the sake of argument, here are a couple of reminders: Compared to dominant organizational models driven by capitalist logic, the Free Food Store is an intriguing case of a small scale 'alternative economy' and an entry point for doing socially relevant research as a critical scholar (Dunne et al, 2008). With a social agenda tackling challenges of food poverty, food waste and sustainability, the shop was built on noncapitalist and solidarity practices prioritizing community well-being, such as giving food away for free to meet people's needs, non-monetary exchange relations and collective volunteer labour – all in all, presenting an opportunity to consider how the economy can be organized differently.

Zanoni et al argue that engaging with such community attempts 'offers [an] alternative paradigm for "other" critical research, from which we can start becoming "other" critical scholars' (2017, p 582). Before my fieldwork experience, my research and political action problematizing dominant capitalist relations were confined to the university's boundaries and would take only the form of reading and writing (see also Shukaitis and Graeber, 2007), mainly in idealized theoretical echo chambers built by academics. My scholarly ideas, considering the role of alternative organizations in driving social change, were formulaic and mostly abstract. Therefore, as I explain in this chapter, my engagement with the community initiative opened a new path through which I encountered new organizational practices, postcapitalist theories and alternative critical scholarship modalities aligning research, pedagogy and activism. It was a 'fundamental shift' in my praxis as an academic (Zanoni et al, 2017, p 583), paving the way to become an-Other critical scholar bringing together practice-based and theory-informed knowledge(s) about day-to-day social transformation.

I call for reconfiguring the 'norms of academic scholarship' (Brewis and Bell, 2020, p 534) with an activist agenda that priorities social change. This kind of research practice is a challenge to a particular understanding of scholarship that is disillusioned with the 'publish or perish' neoliberal logic and that unnecessarily reinforces theoretical rigour over relevance more and more. Hence, this chapter is part of ongoing conversations about transforming our scholarship (Contu, 2020), changing the role critique can play (Prichard and Alakavuklar, 2019) and identifying our research locale for social justice (Weatherall, 2021). As an outcome, I demonstrate how 'bridging' can be a case of 'activist performativity' that transforms research practices and researcher identity, contributes to critical pedagogy and supports community work.

I also hope to inspire my colleagues – against the backdrop of business schools haunted by capitalist ideology (Kociatkiewicz et al, 2021) and mimicking private enterprise (Fleming, 2020), which eventually alienates us (Alakavuklar et al, 2017) – to engage more with social causes and community organizations and their practices. Hence, through activist performativity and doing socially meaningful and relevant research (Tourish, 2020), we can take our intellectual freedom back from the neoliberal business schools imposing a particular scholarship (Jones et al, 2020).

Community solutions

One customer asked Mary, the founder/director, whether we should consider this kind of community solution radical, as 'a socialist act in a capitalist system', given that the shop provides free food. In terms of scholarly interests, the question for me was: can communities and their organizational practices be the new 'locale' for our critical research and radical enough for social change? DeFilippis et al (2006) posit that within their own constraints, community organizations can host attempts at social change. Some other commentators claim that grassroots initiatives constitute the living laboratories of social innovation (Seyfang and Smith, 2007). It is also argued that they play essential caring and solidarity roles for communities (Gómez et al, 2019). Therefore, while the Free Food Store might be a market-compatible community solution and may even rely on the surplus produced by capitalist dynamics, there are perhaps not socialist but alternative practices (that is, in relation to non-monetary exchange relations, volunteer labour, free giving of food, solidarity) which can shed light on ways of organizing economy and society differently. Furthermore, through various other activities, such as documentary screenings and hosting social gatherings, the Free Food Store acts as an intermediary of community development, raising awareness and mobilization concerning food waste and sustainability (Levkoe and Wakefield, 2011; Broad, 2016).

While I could see that the Free Food Store decommodifies the economic relationship between labour and food and offers an alternative way of self-organizing at the margins to sustain the community (Chapter 4), I was puzzled by the limits of this initiative. I ask Mary a similar question – how would she intervene to address the systemic and structural problem of food waste and food poverty? I had hoped to hear a detailed and radical analysis from this first-hand witness. However, her argument is simple and straightforward (as discussed in Chapter 2): "It may be a fatalistic view, but instead of looking at what we can't do, we've been looking at what we can do with the Free Food Store."

While Mary's motivation is of value in addressing the moral and environmental issues about surplus food and food waste, her 'fatalistic view' sheds light on the ethics and politics of the Free Food Store. As I have argued, the Free Food Store – by hosting quite a diverse group of volunteers (that is, Pākehā, Māori, international residents, disabled people, students, academics, professionals, people who are retired and people who are unemployed and being open to anyone (that is, not using means-testing) – is a charity organization that helps members of the local community meet their basic needs without politically addressing the big questions of structural inequalities and social injustices (see Chapter 3). At the same time, there is diversity among volunteers, with clear differences based on profession and class (for example, there were architects, pensioners, social workers, academics, administration officers and students) and customers. Some volunteers struggle to find regular jobs or are on benefit schemes; some also visit the shop as customers. The visibility of the customers queuing in front of the shop is another discussion point among organizational actors. Despite the shop offering a dignified experience for customers through unconditional giving of food, the visibility of the queue outside the shop can lead to stigma and feelings of shame (see Chapter 5). Nevertheless, these differences and challenges are neutralized through the notion of community around the shop. From this perspective, the Free Food Store can be seen as a Band-Aid solution in the era of neoliberal responsibilization of communities and welfare states drawing back (Poppendieck, 1998; van Dyk, 2018).

On the other hand, the Free Food Store is more than a simple food aid organization that reproduces power asymmetries. Following previous chapters, three aspects are striking to note: the moral, environmental and economic justification of saving an immense amount of food (that is, 45,000 kilograms of food, the equivalent of NZ$350,000 retail value, monthly); the fact that many local people are given unconditional help (on average, 325 each day – and those customers also support others); and the shop's awareness-raising about recycling food and sustainability as a member of a national network problematizing food waste. Instead of a political agenda bringing committed people together, as argued in Chapter 3, solidarity links are built on a moral basis to support and empower vulnerable community members in difficult economic times through 'transcending material needs, and creating a collective sense of inclusion as an alternative model to market relationships' (Gómez Garrido et al, 2019, p 770). This aspect is visible through the regular customers, who include large single-income families, single parents, people on benefit schemes, people who are homeless, those in precarious work and anyone struggling to make it to the end of the month.

While trying to understand what to do with the complexity of this alternative organization and its transformative potential, I got a comment from my colleague, triggering the questions and self-reflection points I discussed in Chapter 2. As a reminder, presumably reflecting on her previous perception of the academics (arguably dominant in the Aotearoa New Zealand context; see Bridgman, 2007), she told me that I was not like the other academics who stay on the other side of the bridge (referring to the physical location of the university in the region) and do their jobs as academics. For her, I am the one who "crosses the bridge" to work with the community organization, which, she argued, makes me different. While my initial reflections and questions are discussed in Chapter 2, the impact of this comment was greater than that – it changed the way I understand the role of the academy, communities and critical scholars. This comment was the turning point for my fieldwork and my scholarship. It made me realize how the community perceives academics and, more importantly, reminded me of the urgent and pressing need to be more relevant for the actors already doing what they can, within their own capacity, to tackle challenges and change society through their day-to-day practices. I was urged to reconsider the limits of my participant observation (and my role as an academic) if I wanted to go beyond my comfort zone of 'reading and writing' and do more – literally and metaphorically 'crossing the bridge', getting out of echo chambers, leaving behind the anxieties of being an academic that feed the neoliberal academy and perpetuate ranking, assessment, careerism and individualism (Pullen and Rhodes, 2018; Ruth et al, 2018).

Learning to become an-Other critical scholar, and activist performativity

During my engagement with the Free Food Store, I was pushed to be more reflexive about my positionality, limits and expectations as a critical scholar. As a result, my perception of social change, the role of (critical) scholarship and my research and teaching choices crystallized. My research has undergone a fundamental shift and is now focused on actively engaging with and supporting community initiatives and grassroots organizations that embrace bottom-up, postcapitalist/noncapitalist organizational solutions. This involves not only expanding their practical impact but also opening more spaces in scholarly discourse about the value of these practices. Additionally, I am committed to facilitating collaborations with these entities to collectively shape a political agenda that extends within and beyond the academic sphere. My teaching practice is focused more on alternative organizations' transformative potential, economically and politically, emphasizing local community and grassroots organizations and their sustainability practices. I give more details about this transformation in the last section of the chapter.

As a part of this learning experience, Gibson-Graham's (1996) community economies framework and Wright's (2019) discussion on eroding capitalism have been inspirational. While for Wright, simultaneous change attempts from above (through the state and local governing bodies) and from below (through grassroots organizations, unions and community activism) will gradually erode capitalist economic relations with democratic market socialism, Gibson-Graham addresses communities as a source of bottom-up socioeconomic transformation (see Chapter 7). My crossing the bridge introduced me to the potential of community initiatives, the performative impact of research and the possibilities of mutual learning (Weatherall, 2021).

Many community initiatives are located at the heart of social issues and can be natural allies for critical scholars to practice and learn from, and imagine alternatives (Esper et al, 2017; Parker and Parker, 2017), however complex and contradictory these initiatives' positions (Wright, 2012). While some commentators find the impact of these initiatives limited in terms of transforming broader power relations (DeFilippis et al, 2006; Böhm, 2014), they fulfil the needs of communities, (re)organize economic value relations (Eskelinen, 2020) and lead to the construction of alternative economic, ethical and solidarity practices as sources of social change (Gibson-Graham et al, 2013; Broad, 2016; Gómez Garrido et al, 2019). Therefore, as in the case of the Free Food Store, though they may seem fatalistic, these postcapitalist initiatives facilitate social reproduction and community well-being (Chatterton and Pusey, 2020, pp 41–42) by diverging from the dominant ways of organizing the economy and society (Schmid, 2021). As postcapitalist experiments, economic activities at community level lead to the formation of multiple economic subjects (for example, waged worker, unpaid family carer, volunteer) that not only deconstruct capital-o-centric assumptions, practices and subjectivities but also potentially empower individuals and communities to (re)configure social and political relations through self-organizing (Gibson-Graham, 2006; Healy et al, 2020). Hence, community initiatives are inspirational sources of alternative economic practices, from which academics can draw theories and concepts.

Academics can also play a critical role by collaborating and contributing to these community initiatives. The community economies framework (Gibson-Graham and Dombroski, 2020) is emphasized mainly by management and organization scholars to encourage more relevant and performative critical work in business schools (see, for example, King, 2015; Wharerata Writing Group, 2018; Aslan, 2020). Engaging with these community practices as cases of alternative organization helps us construct new academic subjectivities (that is, an-Other critical scholar) that transform how we do critical research to contribute to social change efforts for a socially just and sustainable society (Just et al, 2021). Through these collaborations, performative effects emerge not only for the communities but also for researchers (Gibson-Graham, 2008) – as this book, and specifically this chapter, demonstrates.

As a derivative of such an impact, I propose 'activist performativity' to reconfigure our scholarship with a social change agenda and politicize our critical research further for a more holistic and nuanced understanding. In doing this, I argue that the performativity debate builds on decades-long scholarly conversations about academic activism (Reedy and King, 2019). It also needs to go beyond its own internal 'web of discussions' taking place in the 'ivory tower' (Just et al, 2021, p 92). I follow Fleming and Banerjee's (2016) problematization of business managers as interlocutors for social change and build my proposal on their call to engage with activists and social movements, acknowledge teaching as a political act and using critical/ radical theories as our toolkit.

With this proposal, my intention is not to introduce yet another theoretical exercise that will remain part of academic outputs; on the contrary, it is a call to bring 'activism' back into the critical research practice that indeed has a performative effect in multiple domains, and to promote a holistic social change agenda. This can create impetus and opportunity to go beyond the limits of discursive interventions (Fleming and Banerjee, 2016) and 'instrumental careerism' (Butler and Spoelstra, 2020, p. 425) that boost an 'unhealthy obsession' with theory development based on spotting tiny gaps (Tourish, 2020, p 100). So, how can activist performativity reconfigure our scholarship for social change?

1. It is built on a holistic understanding of 'critical praxis', focusing on acting and doing. It aligns all the scholarly academic functions (Contu, 2020) with an attempt to break down the perceived separation between research, teaching and activism as the locations of struggle (Chatterton et al, 2010). Hence, as an essential component, critical praxis means practising research, teaching and other academic roles with a critical/radical purpose to make a difference both in society and the academy (Fuller and Kitchin, 2004) as part of resistance and challenge to established research practices and neoliberal discourses of impact (Rhodes et al, 2018).
2. It purposefully addresses activist communities and grassroots organizations as close allies, to create a performative effect on different domains. Such allyship constructs a fruitful ground to work with and for community initiatives, leading to material and embodied engagement with the practices of social change efforts, potentially followed by scholarly contributions in the academic sphere.
3. It calls for engagement with day-to-day practices as a source of individual and collective transformation. Therefore, acting and doing with the purpose of social justice have a performative effect on communities' causes and researchers' practices in the university (that is, social impact).

Overall, activist performativity serves as an academic practice aimed at transforming the university and society from within and without while, at the same time, blurring the boundaries between activist practice, research and teaching. It further sensitizes research to the multifaceted societal and structural challenges. As a result, activist engagement built on practice-based knowledge feeds into scholarly reflection and contribution based on theory-informed knowledge, holistically bringing together the sites of struggle for social justice.

Bridging as activist performativity and implications

As mentioned by my colleague at the Free Food Store, traditionally, the university is positioned as distant from the practice in my research context. This physical distance and perceived tension were evident in transdisciplinary gatherings I attended where academics and practitioners shared experiences. For instance, in a conference related to regional food production, each of the academic speakers began their talks with apologies that they did not have the knowledge of 'practitioners'. Also, the questions posed to the academic speakers after their talks were almost hostile – participants were direct and asked the 'so what?' question.

In fact, this tension between academy and practice has been an ongoing conversation in Aotearoa New Zealand. This had come to my attention – before I engaged with the Free Food Store – at the first Social Movements, Resistance and Social Change Conference (SMRSC), which I organized thanks to a small amount of funding from my university (Alakavuklar and Dickson, 2016). Sue Bradford, a former Green Party Member of Parliament and established Left-wing activist, presented her findings about the relationship between academics and activists at this conference and addressed the (mis)perceptions and the perceived distance (Bradford, 2014). This presentation and other conversations during the conference resonated with me. As a critical scholar located in a business school, this was the first time I had felt at home, with all the talks about organizing social change and its challenges from different perspectives in a postcolonial context like Aotearoa New Zealand.

This small conference, initially attended by 50 people, brought together academics, activists, community organizers and policy makers. It was a milestone in my life, and it turned into a significant platform for bridging together different movements and academic activists in Aotearoa New Zealand (Jaques et al, 2016; Taylor, 2016, 2017). Following the first conference, an e-network was established on the Engaged Social Science/ Hui Rangahou Tahi (eSocSci)[1] platform, to build capacity and support the

---

[1]   See the eSocSci website at: https://esocsci.blogs.auckland.ac.nz/

dialogue between social scientists and activists. Meanwhile, in the years that followed, I witnessed the exponential growth of the annual conference thanks to collective efforts and the leading roles of colleagues working in different universities, activists and community organizers. The conferences provided opportunity to build multiple conversations between the Māori movement, unionists, environmentalists, anticapitalists and academics from various disciplines and traditions, to find ways to collaborate and coproduce knowledge and action for social change (History of the SMRSC Conference, 2020).

The distance between research and practice is not a recent phenomenon in the literature, given the discussions about rigour versus relevance (Butler et al, 2015) and the performativity debate in management and organization studies (Cabantous et al, 2016). From a critical point of view, this tension was already explicit in Marx's thesis 11, concerning the philosopher's (read academic's) role – whether this should be understanding and/or changing the world. Hence, bridging can be a taken-for-granted role of the academic activist, with the assumption of gaps (Sutherland, 2012, p 633; Oslender and Reiter, 2015). Yet, through encounters across domains, imaginary bridges can collapse, leading to different performative outcomes with a more holistic approach (Weatherall, 2021). Therefore, in principle, this separation should be problematized as if the social justice struggles can be categorized and as if there are hierarchical differences between the knowledge(s) produced by scholars and activists (Chatterton et al, 2010; Choudry, 2020). This perspective was evident in the care the SMRSC took to refrain from reproducing the perceived distance and its continuous building of dialogue to encourage working together despite different traditions (Taylor, 2016).

In my research context, however, there was indeed a bridge between the university and the city that had to be crossed many times, in reality and in imaginaries. Hence, my fieldwork allowed me to move out of the usual boundaries of research and create spaces to share practices, meanings and assumptions from different domains. My engagement with the Free Food Store organically turned into a bridging practice not only between the university and the community but also between activism (practice), academy (theory) and teaching (pedagogy). In other words, bridging rendered a holistic critical praxis possible.

As a part of bridging, as is known to many organizational ethnographers, daily talks, mundane interactions, interviews, volunteering for different tasks and guest lectures by community members are all opportunities to facilitate learning from shared practices and each other. These were the few but precious moments when, together with community members and students, I could reflect on the value of giving free food, question who gets what in the current food regimes, discuss possibilities of organizing differently and query the role of academics (and the university) in society. My fieldwork facilitated three forms of bridging.

The first form is *bridging activism and research*. From the outset, I designed my research so that I could contribute to the organization's cause (that is, saving surplus food, improving sustainability) with my labour. My research time, secured by my university (which was a privilege), was dedicated to participant observation so that I could work for the organization wholeheartedly and immerse myself in its day-to-day practices while simultaneously studying it. It was also an opportunity to do something as an active citizen at the local level, to engage with and (co-)politicize grand societal challenges (that is, food waste) and figure out ways academics can 'collaborate with' bottom-up initiatives to contribute to efforts towards social change (Prichard, 2015). Leaving my office and isolated (neoliberal) loneliness to change my research locale led to mutual interaction, engagement and learning between the domains of activism and research.

However, there were also 'aha' moments during my engagement with the Free Food Store, which can be considered uncommon encounters (Chatterton, 2006) between community members and me. For instance, I regretfully recall Mary being seemingly (and perhaps understandably) indifferent to my initial findings, which were full of jargon and ambitious theoretical analysis referring to the alternative material, symbolic and political layers of the organization. She said my talk "went completely above her head, like that [animating with her hands that my words and sentences were passing by her face]". I had to acknowledge that though my language and the way I 'critically' explained things were taken for granted by me and the academic world I am embedded in, that was not the case outside that arena. In another instance, John, the shop manager, asked me (given my affiliation with the School of Management) how I could be a management scholar without 'managing' people. This query was another opportunity to reflect on not only the perception of academics 'over there' in the university studying things they do not 'practise' but also the meanings and power attributed to the management function in a non-market environment.

I had to 'learn to walk again' with the community, to establish common ground and, more importantly, create a new (jargon-free) language, style and method of engagement (Chatterton, 2006). My initial response was to go with the flow of the organization and its daily dynamics rather than thinking about my research agenda and researcher role. This approach freed my mind and opened more space for me to get closer to the day-to-day practices of tackling the challenges of food surplus. Moreover, I witnessed their own complexities and difficulties, became a part of their ongoing daily struggles, supported 'what they can do' with my labour and, where possible, carried their voices into my research and teaching (Reedy and King, 2019). I was pushed to think, act, research and live differently, alongside the community members – I was an academic crossing the bridge, noting the structural problem of surplus food, going back to the literature and the university, coming back to the field to find out more about fatalistic noncapitalist practices, leaving academic echo chambers and research questions aside, noticing the limits of imaginary academic selves and considering different languages, priorities and constraints. The Free Food Store and the community organized around it held a mirror to my profession (Weatherall, 2021). I am unsure if my presence had a similar impact on them.

The second form of bridging was *bridging postcapitalism with the critical theoretical toolkit and scholarly writing*. In the case of the Free Food Store, community initiative became the entry point for theorizing about the possibilities of bottom-up social change and checking the relevance of theories against the reality of practice. Therefore, bridging took place between postcapitalist literature, my theoretical toolkit as an organizational scholar and my scholarly writing. By practising volunteer work with community members, I learned more about the relationship between day-to-day practices, change and imaginaries emerging from the diversity of the economy (Gibson-Graham, 1996, 2006). I had the opportunity to see first-hand the impact of societal challenges (that is, food surplus, food waste, food poverty), the community solutions (that is, redistributing free food, meeting the needs of people, caring for the community) and the potential and limitations of alternative organizations 'within, despite and post' capitalism (Chatterton and Pickerill, 2010, p. 486). The Free Food Store is part of the dominant market structure, benefiting from its dysfunction of overproduction and creation of waste. At the same time, contrary to the usual exchange practices, such as money vis-a-vis food, as a part of our daily consumption, it offers an alternative arrangement of giving food for free. Finally, its divergence from capital accumulation and offer of socially useful production for the community's well-being are indicators of a postcapitalist setting.

As a theoretical experiment, the Free Food Store demonstrates the economy's non-monolithic structure, diverse noncapitalist practices (non-wage work, non-monetary exchange) alongside dominant capitalist practices, and decommodified social relations interwoven with food surplus for the sustainability of the community. Furthermore, through the case of the Free Food Store, I was able to draw attention to the issues around dominant economic practices and ways of organizing (for example, top-down organizing, growth motive, consumerism and lack of fair distribution). The Free Food Store and community activism attest to the validity of critical theories of postcapitalism, and provide a complex case regarding the emergence of noncapitalist value relations within the limits and boundary conditions of a community organization.

The third form of bridging was *bridging activism, research and pedagogy*. Bridging multiple domains and communities contributed to my attempts to teach differently with a social and economic transformation perspective as part of my critical praxis. Against the dominant corporate model, I taught about alternative organizations and their potential to question neoliberal capitalism, individualism and competition, to open up new conversations about the way we organize the economy and society (Reedy and Learmonth, 2009). I took my lessons learned about postcapitalist practices, grassroots organizations and community perspectives to management courses to teach about noncapitalist organizing. I also invited John to be a guest lecturer and share his perspective on societal challenges and how the Free Food Store is organized around community well-being. He emphasized the voluminous amount of surplus food that would become waste if not rescued, and the impact of food waste on the environment. He explained how the Free Food Store is an organization for the community by the community to support those who need food. Students had the opportunity to learn first-hand from John about the issue of poverty amid abundance and the critical caring role community organizations can play against the backdrop of the capitalist economy that creates the problem in the first place. I also encouraged them to 'cross the bridge' and visit the shop as a customer to enjoy a free sandwich, to see an alternative organizational setting with their own eyes. By drawing cases and arguments from the day-to-day practices of the Free Food Store, I attempted to problematize and politicize 'business as usual' management education.

It should be noted that the domains of activism, research and pedagogy do not have clear-cut boundaries. Bridging is a continuous ethical and political struggle to navigate these perceived boundaries and make sense of our role as critical scholars in blurring the lines while learning and testing the limits of the same boundaries. It is a question of who we see as allies, who we work with and whether we reproduce power relations in the process of bridging (Bristow and Robinson, 2018). Therefore, my bridging attempt should be considered 'in relation to others' (Cunliffe, 2008, p 128) within the ethics and politics of the Free Food Store . As mentioned earlier, essentially, learning to go with the flow as a member of the organization, being open and building trust with my 'colleagues' helped me navigate my positionality. While gaining ethical approval from my university was to some extent a bureaucratic exercise, that process meant I was attuned to the power differences and the potential impact of my research at the food shop. Hence, from the beginning of my fieldwork, I did my best to be transparent to all in terms of who I was as a researcher (a middle-class, non-native international academic out of his comfort zone), why I was doing volunteer work (to find out how the Free Food Store operates) and how I was carrying out my research (working with them, taking notes, keeping anonymity, principally doing no harm). Completing tasks together, having sincere chats and mostly listening to others and being discreet helped me build rapport and establish a sense of familiarity and security with the diverse group of volunteers. While this process took time,[2] as far as I am concerned, the perception my colleagues at the shop had of me gradually shifted from 'the curious academic from the other side' to an engaged insider involved in the organization's activities like any other volunteer, under the guidance of Mary and John (Cunliffe and Karunanayake, 2013). This shift (that is, becoming one of the volunteers) was not easy; however, it facilitated an in-depth understanding of the inequalities, tensions and contradictions emerging from this context.

And, you may ask, my dear reader, so what?

Drawing on my transformative and challenging fieldwork experience, I want to offer a more radical positioning concerning how our critical scholarship in business schools matters to us and others. As I have found myself on a new journey to become an-Other critical scholar, there are lessons learned which can incite and encourage my colleagues to reconfigure and perform our scholarship differently. Before concluding, I should note that I was fortunate and privileged; my engagement took place thanks to the dedicated research time provided by the university and the support of both community members and colleagues. Nevertheless, it is impossible to fully know the implications of my engagement, despite my best intentions (Maxey, 1999). The bottom line is my working at the Free Food Store along with other members was based on offering my labour at a material level, and this may have had a modest impact. I am also not sure whether this experience can be considered 'going native' – that is, whether I lost my scientific purpose and fully embraced the values and assumptions of my colleagues. Even though, as a volunteer, I may have become an insider, it is possible that I moved beyond going native so that I could build bridges as a form of activist performativity.

Concerning my experience, there are two outcomes which can be a source of inspiration and provocation, primarily to readers working in universities. 'Bridging domains' is a critical learning that can be considered a form of activist performativity and an academic activist modality. It creates an opportunity for critical praxis to harness the transformative potential of multiple domains within a holistic perspective. Bridging also leads to a cross-fertilization of practices and assumptions for making an impact in different spheres – activism, research, teaching, working with communities. It pushes researchers to engage with Other practices to understand and comprehend the socioeconomic relations, emerging subjectivities and alternative imaginaries that can contribute to individual, collective and organizational transformation. While bridging may imply a perceived separation of domains

---

[2]   I did my first interview after five months of engagement with the Free Food Store.

to be problematized (Weatherall, 2021), metaphorically it invites us to reflect on where we stand as critical scholars, what kind of bridges we build, how many times we cross different bridges as a part of our scholarship, and why.

Additionally, I propose 'activist performativity' as a research practice that targets and prioritizes community initiatives and grassroots organizations as allies to do socially relevant and meaningful research, potentially contributing to social change efforts. Within the boundary conditions of doing critical work in business schools (Ratle et al, 2020; Parker, 2021), activist performativity becomes an an–Other opportunity to do research differently. Nevertheless, against the background of continuous attacks on academic freedom and critical theory in higher education institutions today, activist performativity should not be taken merely as an individual attempt to be relevant to communities 'out there', but as an epistemological and political proposal to build other bridges between collective struggles and alliances within and beyond the university to construct a critical mass. Hence, given its social change agenda, activist performativity cannot be separated from the broader collective critical work and resistance at the neoliberal academy, but should be considered part and parcel of other academic activist engagements (Contu, 2018; Rhodes et al, 2018; Dar et al, 2021; Grosser, 2021). Activist performativity, in that sense, means working towards becoming the change we want to make with the emergence of new (academic) subjectivities and promotion of alternative research practices that challenge and push the orthodoxy of the business schools and society – of course, within the opportunities and limitations we have, recognising all the risks, struggles and failures involved (Callahan and Elliott, 2019).

Now, after my fieldwork experience and engagement with the SMRSC conferences, working in a different institutional setting in the Netherlands my journey of becoming an–Other critical scholar continues with new challenges. I try to follow principles of activist performativity and bridging domains, as in the case of constructing a transdisciplinary postcapitalist network, including activists and academics, for longer-term collective action and more sustained impact (Anders Utrecht[3]); podcasting with network members as a form of coproduction of knowledge; and linking this network with a recently launched master's programme (Organising Social Impact[4]) centred on activism, for which I have the coordinator role. At the time of writing, the network hosts 15 local grassroots organizations tackling societal challenges such as social inclusion, sustainable food, the commodification of art and culture, and environmental protection. It facilitates dialogue between academics from different disciplines (organization studies, sustainability

---

[3] See the 'About us' page at: https://andersutrecht.nl/en/
[4] See the programme webpage at: www.uu.nl/en/masters/organising-social-impact

science, media and communication), encourages collaboration between scholars and activists concerning sustainability transformation in the city through workshops and research, and promotes interorganizational partnerships. To date, seven podcast episodes, each hosting discussion by two different organizational representatives and an academic on the role of grassroots organizations in sustainability transformation, are publicly available to inform interested parties and create awareness about bottom-up sustainability practices.[5] Students of the new master's programme are doing their engaged fieldwork in some of these organizations. To bring theory and praxis together, the students actively engage with and contribute to the organizations' activities (as an alternative to a more detached short-term extractivist data collection exercise), reflect on organizational social impact practices and use these experiences as input for the programme's courses and their dissertations.

As scholarly and practical knowledges converse in this network, the academics and students work as critically engaged partners to activate and contribute to ongoing processes of social change. Hence, an alternative and holistic impact paradigm, different from the metrics and rankings that dominate in the academy, is offered to become an an-Other critical scholar bridging the academy and grassroots activism and bringing people from both sides together to work towards urban sustainability. The university plays a critical role as an anchor institution to keep the relations vibrant and the mutual learning possible over the longer term (I return to this in Chapter 7). In this work that constructs a new locale for our critical research, the scope of working 'with' communities has expanded and moved towards a more collective transdisciplinary initiative to create a broader and sustained impact on research, teaching, community initiatives and society. Without my engagement with the Free Food Store and the limitations I encountered, my current academic work would not be possible, nor would I be the same person.

To conclude, echoing Contu, I wonder whether, as critical scholars in business schools, we can indeed change 'the terms of academia and that of ourselves as academics' (2020, p 754). Will we stay on the other side of the bridge with the risks of more isolation, individualization, competition and alienation (Fleming, 2020)? Or, instead, will we contribute to the multitude of efforts towards social change taking place every day through daily practices here and there? Can we 'build new bridges' to take up the challenges of working with and for communities, and do socially relevant and meaningful research with our critical praxis? I leave the metaphor of bridging and the question of activist performativity here to imagine more

---

[5]   The podcast episodes can be found at: https://andersutrecht.nl/en/andersutrecht-voice/

possibilities of becoming an-Other critical scholar together, and to spark more conversation for a collective political agenda within and beyond the academy. And, my dear reader, considering the various roles you possess, as I asked in Chapter 1, are you prepared to join me in this challenge? Whether you are a student, a colleague, a community organizer or a policy maker, can we work together towards creating a more socially just and ecologically sustainable society, guided by and actively embracing alternative practices?

7

Still in Search of Alternatives:
Do We Have an Answer Yet?

My dear reader, have I kept your attention up to this point of the book? You may have sensed ups and downs throughout the book, similar to my experiences of fieldwork. Despite my best intentions, I feel like I cannot eliminate my anxiety. Have I explained well enough? Are the terms clear? Is the writing as accessible as I imagined? There are probably many interesting scholarly conversations I have missed, and, most likely, I would have delved into more in-depth discussions if I had more time. But, in a world where resources are finite, this is the best I can do with the purpose of doing academic work differently.

Writing this book has been a difficult journey that cut across three countries and two continents, moving houses seven times in seven years and going through (post-)pandemic conditions in the country I was trying to settle in. As exemplified in previous chapters, the personal and the political inevitably interweave in my research, and my context has transformed who I am as a researcher. Coming out of a relatively mainstream business school in Turkey with a PhD in Business Administration, I found an institutional home in Aotearoa New Zealand that supported my engagement with a small community organization. As I explored critical theories and their potential for social change, I found myself among the most exciting conversations about bringing academic and activist voices together. While I witnessed first-hand the perception of distance between these two groups, I began imagining (and working towards) an alternative academy that purposefully collaborates with bottom-up initiatives for social change. This strategic direction ended up with my being part of a transdisciplinary network in the Netherlands, having a new academic home and embracing the agenda of critical organization studies.

In this chapter, I present my final reflections and lessons learned, while my search for alternatives continues. This is my last chance in this journey (with you) to say whether I can provide any specific answers in relation to my fieldwork at the Free Food Store. In other words, what have I found delving into organizing food, faith and freedom in a small charity shop? Have I been pushing, unnecessarily, to see alternatives in this community initiative, or have I found fertile ground from which to imagine alternatives?

I must begin by confessing what is already known to many ethnographers – I had some assumptions before my fieldwork. And these changed during the course of my fieldwork. This is not that unexpected, but I need to mention that the concepts I had in my mind before starting fieldwork did not fit with the perceptions of my colleagues at the Free Food Store. Reflecting on this now, perhaps I wanted to see politically committed people who already problematized capitalist relations and social and economic externalizations, and deliberately argued for and prefigured an alternative free shop. Instead, I have realized that paths of people from all walks of life with different motivations intersect in this tiny shop 'to do something good' for the community they belong to. While rescuing food might seem like a kind of activism, my interactions and conversations showed me that community members did not consider their actions politically motivated but primarily talked about how meeting the needs of the people is essential. However, perhaps it is in their practices that we can see the seeds of transformation, as argued by Holloway (2002). Regardless of their political motivation, the Free Food Store facilitates doing and acting (the 'power-to-do'; Holloway, 2002, p 2), which are already embedded in the social and the community. This can also be considered a case of ethical community economy that transforms the relations and subjectivities of the members as they work towards meeting people's needs (Gibson-Graham et al, 2013). Some will argue it is a kind of social and solidarity economy integrating economic, social, environmental and cultural objectives (Utting, 2015). Some others would critically argue that all this good will unintentionally serves the interests of the economic elite due to the political-economic organization of our society. They would say that the availability of sustenance and the social reproduction of care mechanisms at the community level encourage people to continue working within the same economic structures, reproducing inequalities (Bhattacharya, 2017). What am I to do with these different claims, as each has something to offer to explain what I saw at the Free Food Store?

Moreover, getting involved in the world of food rescue and charity made me realize that the issues are messier and more complex than I had initially thought – take the neoliberal policies that are transforming a country, the increase in food poverty, the rise of food insecurity, the capitalist and noncapitalist/alternative food regimes, the immense amount of food surplus potentially becoming waste, the religious narratives, the political narratives, the role of academia and academics, the interrelationship between theory and practice. You might ask: But isn't it your job as an academic to make sense of all these complexities? Fair question! I would not claim that I have all the answers, as there are multiple claims on the 'truth'; mine is only one perspective, informed by some critical theories and observations. Does this mean I was pretty naive or unprepared for such complex engagement? How could I know about all the complexities before engaging with them? Is there a way to connect the dots or untangle the messiness?

In their highly influential article, inspired by Eve Kosofsky Sedgwick,[1] Gibson-Graham argue about 'weak theory'. According to them:

> The practice of weak theorising involves refusing to extend explanation too widely or deeply, refusing to know too much. Weak theory could not know that social experiments are doomed to fail or destined to reinforce dominance; it could not tell us that the world economy will never be transformed by the disorganised proliferation of local projects. ... The choice to create weak theory about diverse economies is a political/ethical decision that influences what kind of worlds we can imagine and create, ones in which we enact and construct rather than resist (or succumb to) economic realities. (2008, p 619)

A weak theory approach is a non-essentialist engagement with the empirical reality without knowing and arguing for a predetermined result or truth. Hence, the weak theory approach is open to the possibility of multiple interpretations and trajectories concerning social change. It helps us 'describe, appreciate, connect and analyze, identifying strengths to build on and constraints to work around' (Gibson-Graham and Dombroski, 2020, p 9). Therefore, it is an ontological position of 'reading for economic difference' (Gibson-Graham, 2020; see also Burke and Shear, 2014) in the given historical and political context without assuming a concrete law of change (Gibson-Graham, 2006, pp 49–50). I see the relevance of weak theory to identify and theorize further about the strengths of the Free Food Store, promising a mobilization at community level, helping and supporting people unconditionally and self-organizing without promising a grand transformation.

Such an attempt at theorizing also means acknowledging the factors surrounding and shaping the strengths in this specific context – a charity form driven by faith in a neoliberal context with its own power relations. In doing this, I found mediation helpful as a critical and analytical concept. I used it liberally and out of its dominant Marxist orientation. In this way, I could explain how faith-based (Chapter 3), economic (Chapter 4) and power-laden (Chapter 5) day-to-day practices and discourses mediate and

---

[1]   One of the pioneers and most influential theorists of queer studies, problematizing monolithic representations and hegemonic formations such as gender binary thinking.

bind them with relations and organizational actors in the case of the Free Food Store. In the following, based on the central premises of weak theory, I connect the dots and reflect on what these connections offer us in terms of imagining alternatives and how academics can play a role in this process.

Organizing food, faith and freedom through symbolic, economic and political layers

The role of faith and religion in the Free Food Store are critical as they are embedded in the formation of the organization's identity since its foundation. While the Free Food Store has no evangelical purpose to convert people to Christianity, faith plays a role in the symbolic structure of the organization. While only some volunteers share this view of the symbolic structure, the organization's discursive and material practices explicitly and implicitly facilitate the mediation of organizational relations and the network of food aid charities and associations. Being open to all with no judgment and unconditional love are the apparent signifiers of religious altruism to tackle the food poverty issue in a world that continuously produces food waste in a food-rich country. However, given the structural dynamics, this altruism and caring for the community have their own limits. As the contradiction between food surplus, food waste and food deprivation shows, there is indeed enough food for everyone; yet it is not fairly distributed. The scarcity of food is an arbitrary economic construct stemming from the current organization of exchange and value relations. The global agrifood system, driven by corporate profit over people and the natural environment, significantly contributes to this structural problem (Howard, 2016; Böhm et al, 2020). Therefore, it is not an issue that can be tackled at the individual or community level (see also Holt-Gimenez, 2019). Mary, the founder/director, made a deliberate choice to act within the boundaries of what is already available.

This fatalistic view, however, empowered the community through a charity form and mobilized people. While critiques abound concerning the function of the charity in a neoliberal society, this type of organization is not prevented from acting as a food rescue organization that can potentially provide a space for 'socially useful production' (Chatterton and Pusey, 2020). Thus, the community can sustain itself differently without the need for confession of poverty (that is, means-testing) as in the case with food banks and other food charities. What is more, rescuing food contributes not only to a self-sustaining community but also ecological sustainability. Having said that, when it comes to 'big questions', the Free Food Store, driven mainly by a moral imperative, could not escape making a contribution to the depoliticization of economic inequalities. While the mediation of faith has the strength to mobilize the community for its own sake and the environment's sake, I argue that faith inevitably surrendered to neoliberal impositions. Your question, my dear reader, might then be: should they bother with this issue? As Mary simply spoke in terms of saving food from becoming waste and giving it to people in need, perhaps this has never been on their agenda. Acknowledging my predetermined categories (again) and learning from my colleagues at the Free Food Store, I ask: might it be the onerous task of the university to point out such contradictions and challenges? This a question I come back to later in the chapter.

From a diverse economic perspective, this does not mean a grim picture for community initiatives. As a part of useful social production and alternative value relations (Jonas, 2013), the Free Food Store is an exciting case of community organizing that acts in a grey area where capitalist and noncapitalist practices, and material and symbolic relations and institutions, are entangled. This complex entanglement concerns many other alternative forms of organizing as a theoretical puzzle (Parker et al, 2014a). I propose a theoretical opening by focusing on the material economic layer of the organization through food and labour, and demonstrate how use value mediates social relations alternatively, within and to some extent beyond capitalist relations. In conversation with the literature on Marxian value relations, I explain how prevailing economic relations enable an alternative form of organizing that might be seen as parasitic. Relatedly, I explore how economic, symbolic and political relations manifest differently in a diverse economic environment. This is a novel approach to analytically untangle the social relations emerging in this grey area, opening up possibilities for thinking, acting and doing 'economy' differently. Again, while the strengths of 'difference' are welcomed by empowering communities with noncapitalist practices, its own constraints concerning power relations are revealed.

Going further in analyzing power and political relations, in Chapter 5, I used Foucauldian analysis and the dispositive as an analytical and methodological tool (Raffnsøe et al, 2016) to argue what social forces are at play in the context of the Free Food Store. This approach allowed me to go beyond the dichotomist understanding of power/resistance, discursive/material and inside/outside organizational relations, and helped me demonstrate how freedom is exercised positively and negatively through the simultaneous interplay of particular disciplinary mechanisms, enabled and constrained by the Free Food Store. As a result, despite the narrative of being a 'free store', I argue how freedom can be disciplined and contested simultaneously (Villadsen, 2021) in the given context due to the overdetermination of neoliberalism, sustenance, faith and community needs. Through the dispositive, I render visible the mediation of power relations and the interrelationships between macro- and meso-level constructs that shape and structure the discourses and material practices at the Free Food Store.

My engagement with the Free Food Store began with identifying the tensions and potentialities for mobilization around food surplus at community level. As I identified as a critical organization scholar, confronting big questions of poverty amid abundance turned into querying my assumptions about the value of my research and my academic function in such a context (Weatherall, 2021). That is why my work with the Free Food Store has also been transformational in making sense of my 'self' as an academic trying to be an activist. This tension between academic and the activist, reflected in Chapter 2, found its resolution in Chapter 6 in the form of 'critical praxis', 'activist performativity' and 'bridging'. Nevertheless, it is a tentative resolution, since the academic activist identity is always in a dialectical formation. As critical theories and activist practices converse, a synthesis emerges that inevitably shapes and structures the identities of both sides. Therefore, this process is an endless journey of discovering the potential of academic activism in multiple forms, engaging with colleagues from activist circles, learning from them and (co)working towards social change within communities and the university.

The autonomy provided by the academy, with its pluralistic logic, helped me develop an alternative form of critical scholarship, bringing critical pedagogy together with activism and impact. I wanted to go beyond only publishing critical ideas and see the relevance of theory with the practice of social change (and inevitable tensions and potentialities). I had the opportunity to engage with the Social Movements, Resistance and Social Change conferences and witness the mobilization of Māori, environmentalist, feminist, LGBTQI+, unionist and academic activists in Aotearoa New Zealand. The transdisciplinary network of Anders Utrecht was built on this experience in the Netherlands. At the least, it became clear that despite the contested nature of theory, knowledge and the university as an institution, it can still create spaces for collaboration with social change agents. For me, this meant carving out spaces where an academic activist can teach what they study and facilitate bridging such knowledge with social change efforts at multiple levels. This holistic approach is derived from 'critical praxis' (Fuller and Kitchin, 2004), which highlights the primary purpose of social change within the university and society through our academic functions. As an approach, I proposed activist performativity, prioritizing working with activists and with community and grassroots organizations to build a collective political project around critical organization scholarship. While these attempts are still experimental, they are acknowledged in activist circles as equal partnership emerges.

Paradoxes

The book can be read against three paradoxes that cut across organizing food, faith and freedom. Schad et al define paradox as 'a persistent contradiction between interdependent elements' (2016, p 6). The Free Food Store's economic, symbolic and political layers are part of a larger set of interdependent relations, which have unresolvable tensions and contradictions due to their setup.

The first paradox is embedded in the economic ecosystem (Peredo and McLean, 2020), of which the Free Food Store is a part. The global food production value chain, coordinated by multinational corporations, continuously and simultaneously produces food surplus and poverty. Food rescue mobilizations, food banks and food charities play a key role here as intermediaries in solving the problem of poverty, though they rely on the same global corporate structure (Salonen, 2018). Despite their awareness of the challenging socioeconomic context in which members operate, their activities are driven mainly by moral imperatives, and their critical political edge is smoothed out (Watson, 2019). As a result, they inevitably play a role in reproducing the paradox between food surplus, food waste and poverty, which is dominated by neoliberal market relations.

The second paradox builds on the first paradox, between the moral and the political motives for social change. In the case of the Free Food Store, the moral imperative does not become a political movement to change and challenge the economic system; however, it addresses environmental sustainability and empowers the community. There is a moral drive to intervene in the excesses, which creates social and economic value for community members. However, it can also be argued that the priorities of the economic logic and the externalizations are compensated for using the same moral and environmental logic. A political motive would mean challenging and radicalizing such a compensation relation. Theoretically, this can be framed as the domination of the neoliberal market forces over society and humanity (Polanyi, 2001) while the communities develop innovative solutions to tackle challenges created by the same market forces (Seyfang and Smith, 2007).

The third paradox concerns the empowerment of community in the case of the Free Food Store. While the availability of surplus food facilitates a kind of financial assistance for those who cannot make it to the end of the month and empowers them, these people inevitably become part of a subjectification process, which I call 'disciplined freedom'. Despite the abundance of food and the notion of unconditionality, the structurally constructed 'scarcity' becomes a disciplining mechanism through the needs of the Other community members. As Tedmanson et al (2015) argue, the Free Food Store may have a positive emancipatory perspective. However, there can be a dark side to the same practices, potentially reproducing the power relations (Watson and Ekici, 2020).

Where to go from here?

After reading the above, you might ask: Well, Ozan, thanks for all these discussions, but what is the value of this? This question has been with me since the beginning of my fieldwork – if the Free Food Store does represent an alternative organizational model, what should we expect from it? What kind of transformation process should we envision? Are these related to my predetermined concepts, or am I onto something different? This book is a testimony to figuring out (together) what the Free Food Store is about, and I turn to the literature on strategies of social change to provide a better context to position it.

Following the central premise of weak theorizing, I argue that the 'so what' question resides in the potentialities and uncertainties of community organizations tackling societal challenges at the grassroots level. These organizations are not political organizations per se, immediately problematizing the inequalities and externalities capitalist relations create. They do not have a political agenda to intervene in institutional and economic regimes. Despite their noncapitalist 'doing' and 'practising', they do not purposefully prefigure an alternative life (Monticelli, 2021) independent of capitalist relations and pressures, ceaselessly sucking (im)material value out of social reproduction (Hardt and Negri, 2001).

Instead, they do what they can within the given parameters concerning the available resources and the community's well-being. Again, as a part of weak theorizing, I cannot claim that these attempts turn into concrete long-term solutions for many. However, I can 'describe' and 'reinforce' the solidarity, community belonging and sustainability transformations as the strengths of such initiatives. Acknowledging the limitations of local solutions, I can further emphasize how communities can self-govern and empower their members against financial and social pressures.

Going back to Erik Olin Wright (2019), despite its entanglement with capitalist relations (Chapter 4), the Free Food Store can be considered a form of social and solidarity economy organized around the community's needs. For Wright, such (a)political community attempts, which 'may not have generally been crystallized into systematic anticapitalist ideologies, but nevertheless [have] a coherent logic' (2019, p 51), are considered a strategy for escaping capitalism, acknowledging the complexity of societal transformation and the requirement for a multitude of actions. Hence, 'escaping capitalism typically involves avoiding political engagement and certainly collectively organized efforts at changing the world' (Wright, 2019, p 52). However, Wright argues that such social economies contribute to 'interstitial transformations' that

> seek to build new forms of social empowerment in capitalist society's niches and margins, often where they do not seem to pose any immediate threat to dominant classes and elites. … The central theoretical idea is that building alternatives on the ground in whatever spaces are possible both serves a critical ideological function by showing

that alternative ways of working and living are possible, and potentially erodes constraints on the spaces themselves. (2012, p 20)

If we adopt this perspective of interstitial transformation with the assumptions of weak theory, the Free Food Store offers us a set of alternative possibilities. However, they are entangled with complex and contradicting socioeconomic relations. Indeed, as products of specific, economic, cultural and political embeddedness, these entanglements and paradoxes both enable and constrain possibilities of social change with, beyond and against the orthodoxy (Böhm et al, 2010).

In this analysis to 'trace multiple dynamics at play' (Gibson-Graham, 2014, p S147), I also refer to the normative foundations of social transformation derived from Wright (2019). He argues for values that should drive the change and be explicit in the practices of alternatives: equality/fairness; democracy/freedom; and community/solidarity. While equality/fairness emphasizes the 'equal access to the material and social means necessary to live a flourishing life' (Wright, 2019, p 10), democracy/freedom highlights 'equal access to the necessary means to participate meaningfully in decisions about things that affect [people's] lives' (p 15) and community/solidarity underscores the importance of cooperation with a commitment to the well-being of others and due to a moral obligation (p 18).

In my last analysis, I begin by recognizing the limitations of the Free Food Store concerning its role in structural change as such constraints should not prevent us from acknowledging the Free Food Store's theoretical and practical experimental value in searching for alternatives. At the least, we do not live in an ideal world, and the Free Food Store is one of the collective attempts that can offer new insights concerning alternative ways of living.

The Free Food Store begins by mobilizing faith to deal with food poverty. This mobilization renders a sustainable and dignified community support system for community well-being. In doing so, it is not a primary concern whether the food is fairly redistributed, whether the capitalist food regimes should be challenged or even whether the nutritional values of food are considered. Within the given specific context, with the available resources, the Free Food Store is driven by a moral critique about the excesses of food waste and helping those who need food. This attempt builds solidarity links at the individual and community levels (whatever the motivation of other volunteers and other organizations involved) and creates awareness about sustainability (Gómez Garrido et al, 2019). Therefore, in conversation with Wright, we see the essential tenets of community and solidarity.

The food poverty that the faith motive was triggered to solve and the solidarity links that were to be built were also a response to the neoliberal transformation of the country. However, the macroeconomic policy changes come with discourses and practices that lay the ground for blaming individuals for their failures and the claims that poverty results from the individual's choices. As faith-based solutions act like intermediary problem-solvers between the corporate food producers and those in poverty, the mobilization of faith is inevitably subsumed and neutralized by neoliberal discourses and practices.

On the other hand, within the same community organizing, the seeds of a noncapitalist society are sown. If food is abundant, why not give it free without any condition or monetary exchange? Hence, again, there are potentialities to think about in a society without money, based on bartering or gift-giving relations (Rehn, 2014) and transforming monetary relations built on exchange value. Free giving and unconditionality are challenges to the dominant socioeconomic capitalist relations, which prioritize competition and reproducing inequalities. Whoever you are, if you come to the shop, you are eligible to access the food that is available that day. Following Wright, the shop creates spaces of equality and fairness by facilitating access to food to meet needs. While this is critical for the community, as mentioned earlier, at a macro level, paradoxically, the sustainability of free giving relies on the inequalities and externalities of the economic system.

When it comes to democracy and freedom, the limitations of the Free Food Store become much more visible. As there are attempts to create awareness about food waste, there are no conversations about democratizing food production, distribution and consumption practices, or facilitating people to participate in decision-making. These demands for democracy may threaten the interests of the global agrifood companies and retailers at the macro level, which the Free Food Store (in)directly relies on. While freedom (of choice) becomes disciplined at the organizational level owing to the interplay of multiple social forces, at societal level, neoliberal practices, however contested they are, shape and structure the capacity to exercise such freedom, which is dependent on accessing and accumulating financial resources.

As it is, within these limitations, the Free Food Store already improves the lives of communities and presents a case of 'care' for communities. As a miniature economic experiment, it hosts alternative practices to think differently about food, faith and freedom. Then, following Wright, the Free Food Store can play its role as part of the interstitial transformation despite the critiques from the radical Left:

> Activists on the left, especially those on the radical left, often regard these kinds of locally oriented, community-based initiatives as not being very political, because they do not always involve direct confrontation with political power. This is a narrow view of politics. Interstitial strategies to create real utopias involve showing that another world is possible by building it in the spaces available, and then pushing against the state and public policy to expand those spaces. For many people

these kinds of interstitial initiatives also have the advantage of generating immediate, tangible results in which each person's contribution clearly matters. (2012, p 22)

The community members may have different perspectives on the role and function of the Free Food Store. In an ideal world, with some critical speculation, I could also imagine that the Free Food Store, as a community organization, can be inspirational, given the possibility of going beyond a moral critique of 'food waste' towards political mobilization against food poverty by pushing against neoliberal policies. However, perhaps that would not be the Free Food Store as told in this book.

Going back to the premises of weak theory, for a realist representation, the Free Food Store can be considered an ontological space of construction and enacting differences with multiple openings (Healy, 2009; Burke and Shear, 2014). In the ongoing search for alternatives that potentially promote equality/fairness, democracy/freedom and community/solidarity, there are lessons to be drawn from the Free Food Store, since it shows that there are spaces for alternative, cultural and political practices next to and beyond the orthodoxy. If we begin with the assumptions that the status quo is (and should be) contested, that there will always be an endless struggle between multiple forces and institutions, and that there are always alternative forms to work with (Burrell, 2022), the Free Food Store with its present paradoxes and potentialities plays a critical ideological function. Through this function, the possibilities of reversing dominant assumptions, beliefs and practices emerge, allowing for learning from their constraints and ways of imagining society and the economy differently. In the specific case of the Free Food Store, the mediation of faith, the use value of food and labour, and the particular form of power relations facilitate an imaginary of alternative organizing in a diverse economic setting.

So, my dear reader, there is an answer to the question in the title of this chapter. Between multiple claims about how we can and should organize for a just society, the Free Food Store is one of the cases to delve into the complexities of organizing differently through food, faith and freedom, which informs and enriches our theoretical and political imaginaries. My answer here is not definite, and it is bounded by the contextuality of the Free Food Store and by the limits of my own imagination. However, such cases are open for discovery, exploration and experimentation through weak theorizing and (co-)imagining with those who already generate change and impact on the ground.

No perfect 'alternative organization' exists, as organizing is always imbued with politics and power relations, and emerges within, beyond and against dominant capitalist relations (Parker et al, 2014a; Del Fa and Vasquez, 2019). Organizations already function in various ways within the diversity of organizational practices and social relations. Therefore, the search for alternatives should begin with recognizing organizations' limitations, finding ways of working around constraints and strengthening their potential for transforming the status quo, perhaps expecting no immediate results. While food, faith and freedom were my entry points to claim the not so perfect alternative-ness of the Free Food Store, there are multiple entry points to imagining alternatives as we delve into their symbolic, economic and political relations. I want to close the book by returning to the university as a partner and anchor institution in searching, practising and imagining alternatives.

(Co-)imagining in the search for alternatives: the university as an anchor institution for social change

At this time of multiple societal challenges – military conflict, the impact of the COVID-19 pandemic, climate change and rising inequalities – the university is ridden with conflict. Reflecting its multiple and historical relations with the state, market actors, individual citizens, specific communities and grassroots organizations, today's university hosts multiple contradictory logics and legacies (Kavanagh, 2009). While some expect the university to educate the future workforce for the market (Prokou, 2008), others consider it the temple of objective, 'evidence-based' scientific knowledge that should inform policies at various levels. Yet others plead for a university that plays a 'critical' role in progressive change (Giroux, 2014).

Following Giroux, and concerning the role of critical scholars in the face of grand challenges, we need to study, imagine and promote alternatives more than ever. I argue that this should be done with those working towards social change. As shown in this book, there are multiple possibilities for not only theorizing but also (co-)imagining and working together towards socially and ecologically just societies with various bottom-up grassroots and community organizations.

By building transdisciplinary networks, collaborating on research projects, doing engaged fieldwork, organizing guest lectures and workshops, and codesigning curricula and education programmes, the opportunities are there to be taken, despite all the pressures of the contested neoliberal logic in the university. Such collaborations not only create a fertile ground but also facilitate recognition of the performative ontology of alternative economies and organizations (Gibson-Graham, 2014). Learning from each other improves our thinking and practices so that we can go beyond decolonizing the imaginaries dominated by capital-o-centrism, growth ideology or quick and technical solutions for social change (Feola, 2019; Ergene et al, 2021).

Gümüsay and Reinecke (2022) emphasize the importance of research on 'real utopias' and legitimizing their practices so that social change can be co-created from the margins. They also propose 'imagining' as a way forward to theorize for the future:

> We believe that there is another way of researching the future that goes beyond the search for existing empirical alternatives: feeding forward soci(et)al change through acts of imagination about the future. Imagination refers to the ability to form pictures in one's mind of something that cannot be immediately sensed or that has not been previously perceived: the irreal, unreal, and surreal. Imagining is making the absent present. However, the validity of theories based on imagination cannot be tested against the empirical present and might be deemed pseudo-science. Such acts of imagination, therefore, require a new methodological toolkit to achieve speculative rigor. As an academic approach, we need disciplined imagination not only of what is feasible and probable, but also of what is desirable. (Gümüsay and Reinecke, 2022, p 238)

I wonder if the university and academics can facilitate co-imagining the alternative futures with the contribution of grassroots and community organizations, and if the university can become an anchor institution for social change as an equal partner to those who tackle societal challenges on the ground. As argued by Parker (2023), this requires reformulating and restructuring the university and academic work to co-create infrastructures to enable doing academic work differently. This task may not be easy given the established traditions of the institution, acting as if it is the ultimate guardian and the temple of 'knowledge and truth'. However, the crises we live through are so pressing that the university cannot continue with 'business as usual'; we witness calls from various constituencies for the university and science to be more transformative and activist (Norgard and Bengsten, 2021), though this also comes with the risks of responsibilization and co-optation of academic activism (Macfarlane, 2021). Perhaps this is the next challenge for me and those who want to become an-Other critical scholar through 'activist performativity' to transform the university and society by creating and bridging infrastructures of co-imagining.

At the very end of the book, are you still with me, my dear reader? This is where my story ends (or it is from where it will continue) with food, faith and freedom, with some answers but still some questions. Can we (co-)imagine and work towards alternatives, accepting that there are multiple unknown trajectories, openness and inherent tensions ahead?

Appendix

Table A.1: Interviewees

Relation to the Free Food Store (Pseudonym)	Length of association with the Free Food Store (at the time of fieldwork)	Gender
Director/founder (Mary)	4 years	Female
Shop manager (John)	1 year, 6 months	Male
Volunteer 1 (Adele)	1 year, 3 months	Female
Volunteer 2 (Rose)	8 months	Female
Volunteer 3 (Alex)	1 year, 7 months	Female
Volunteer 4 (Emma)	1 year, 6 months	Female
Volunteer 5 (Elaine)	1 year	Female
Volunteer 6 (Oliver)	4 years	Male
Volunteer 7 (Sarah)	10 months	Female
Volunteer 8 (Brigit)	11 months	Female
Volunteer 9 (Lara)	10 months	Female
Volunteer 10 (Riley)	6 months	Male
Supplier 1: Warehouse manager	Daily donations since February 2015	Male
Supplier 2: Quality manager	Occasional donations for over a year	Female
Supplier 3a: Store manager	Daily donations for over 3 years	Male
Supplier 3b: Head of corporate affairs		Male

References

Adler, P.S., Forbes, L.C. and Willmott, H. (2007) 'Critical management studies', *Academy of Management Annals*, 1(1): 119–179.

Alakavuklar, O.N. (2012) *Yönetsel kontrole direncin ahlakı*, Unpublished PhD thesis, Dokuz Eylul University.

Alakavuklar, O.N. (2014) 'Challenging the dominant paradigm: critical management knowledge for humanistic management', in N. Lupton and M. Pirson (eds) *Humanistic Perspectives on International Business and Management*, London: Palgrave Macmillan, pp 25–38.

Alakavuklar, O.N. (2017) 'Labour of becoming a (critical) management scholar: ambivalences, tensions and possibilities', *ephemera*, 17(3): 641–651.

Alakavuklar, O.N. (2020) '(Re)imagining the activist academy', in A. Pullen, J. Helin and N. Harding (eds) *Writing Differently: Dialogues in Critical Management Studies*, Vol 4, Bingley, UK: Emerald Publishing, pp 193–207.

Alakavuklar, O.N. and Parker, M. (2011) 'Responsibility and the local: the prospects for critical management in Turkey', *Critical Perspectives on International Business*, 7(4): 326–342.

Alakavuklar, O.N. and Dickson, A. (2016) 'Social movements, resistance and social change in Aotearoa/New Zealand: an intervention for dialogue, collaboration and synergy', *Kōtuitui: New Zealand Journal of Social Sciences Online*, 11(2): 83–88.

Alakavuklar, O.N. and Alamgir, F. (2018) 'Ethics of resistance in organisations: a conceptual proposal', *Journal of Business Ethics*, 149(1): 31–43.

Alakavuklar, O.N., Dickson, A. and Stablein, R. (2017) 'The alienation of scholarship in modern business schools: from Marxist material relations to the Lacanian subject', *Academy of Management Learning & Education*, 16(3): 454–468.

Albala, K. (ed) (2013) *Routledge International Handbook of Food Studies*, London: Routledge.

Alexander, C. and Smaje, C. (2008) 'Surplus retail food redistribution: an analysis of a third sector model', *Resources, Conservation and Recycling*, 52(11): 1290–1298.

Allen, C. (2016) 'Food poverty and Christianity in Britain: a theological re-assessment', *Political Theology*, 17(4): 361–377.

Appadurai, A. (1988) 'Introduction: commodities and the politics of value', in A. Appadurai (ed) *The Social Life of Things: Commodities in Cultural Perspective*, Cambridge: Cambridge University Press, pp 3–63.

Arendt, H. (1968) *Between Past and Future: Eight Exercises in Political Thought*, New York: Viking Press.

Arvidsson, A. (2009) 'The ethical economy: towards a post-capitalist theory of value', *Capital and Class*, 33(1): 13–29.

Aslan, A. (2020) 'How can critical management studies get out of its ivory tower? Critical performativity and community economies', *Ankara Universitesi, SBF Dergisi*, 75(2): 667–685.

Atkins, P.J. and Bowler, I.R. (2016) *Food in Society: Economy, Culture, Geography*, Abingdon: Routledge.

Atzeni, M. (ed) (2012) *Alternative Work Organizations*, Basingstoke: Palgrave Macmillan.

Baker, G. (2006) 'Freedom', in A. Harrington, B.L. Marshall and H.P. Müller (eds) *Encyclopedia of Social Theory*, London: Routledge, pp 206–207.

Baker, T. and Davis, C. (2018) 'Everyday resistance to workfare: welfare beneficiary advocacy in Auckland, New Zealand', *Social Policy and Society*, 17(4): 535–546.

Barin Cruz, L., Alves, M.A. and Delbridge, R. (2017) 'Next steps in organizing alternatives to capitalism: toward a relational research agenda', *M@n@gement*, 20(4): 322–335.

Berlin, I. (1969) *Four Essays on Liberty*, Oxford: Oxford University Press.

Bhattacharya, T. (ed) (2017) *Social Reproduction Theory: Remapping Class, Re-Centering Oppression*, London: Pluto.

Böhm, S. (2014) 'Book review symposium: JK Gibson-Graham, Jenny Cameron and Stephen Healy, take back the economy: an ethical guide for transforming our communities', *Sociology*, 48(5): 1055–1057.

Böhm, S., Dinerstein, A.C. and Spicer, A. (2010) '(Im)possibilities of autonomy: social movements in and beyond capital, the state and development', *Social Movement Studies*, 9(1): 17–32.

Böhm, S., Spierenburg, M. and Lang, T. (2020) 'Fruits of our labour: work and organisation in the global food system', *Organization*, 27(2): 195–212.

Boncori, I. (2022) *Researching and Writing Differently*, Bristol: Policy Press.

Boyacigiller, N.A. and Adler, N.J. (1991) 'The parochial dinosaur: organizational science in a global context', *Academy of Management Review*, 16(2): 262–290.

Bracewell-Worrall, A. (2018, 23 April) 'Food grants: number of New Zealanders getting help with basics continues rising', *Newshub*, retrieved from: www.newshub.co.nz/home/politics/2018/04/food-grants-num ber-of-new-zealanders-getting-help-with-basics-continues-rising.html

Bradford, S. (2014) *A Major Left Wing Think Tank in Aotearoa: An Impossible Dream or a Call to Action?* Unpublished PhD thesis, Auckland University of Technology.

Brewis, D. and Bell, E. (2020) 'Provocation essays editorial: on the importance of moving and being moved', *Management Learning*, 51(5): 533–536.

Bridgman, T. (2007) 'Assassins in academia? New Zealand academics as critic and conscience of society', *New Zealand Sociology*, 22(1): 126–144.

Briner, R.B. and Sturdy, A. (2008) 'Introduction to food, work and organization', *Human Relations*, 61(7): 907–912.

Bristow, A. and Robinson, S. (2018) 'Brexiting CMS', *Organization*, 25(5): 636–648.

Broad, G. (2016) *More than Just Food: Food Justice and Community Change*, Oakland: University of California Press.

Brown, W. (2015) *Undoing the Demos: Neoliberalism's Stealth Revolution*, Cambridge, MA: MIT Press.

Burke, B.J. and Shear, B. (2014) 'Introduction: engaged scholarship for non-capitalist political ecologies', *Journal of Political Ecology*, 21(1): 127–144.

Burrell, G. (2022) *Organization Theory: A Research Overview*, London: Routledge.

Butler, N. and Spoelstra, S. (2014) 'The regime of excellence and the erosion of ethos in critical management studies', *British Journal of Management*, 25(3): 538–550.

Butler, N. and Spoelstra, S. (2020) 'Academics at play: why the "publication game" is more than a metaphor', *Management Learning*, 51(4): 414–430.

Butler, N., Delaney, H. and Spoelstra, S. (2015) 'Problematizing "relevance" in the business school: the case of leadership studies', *British Journal of Management*, 26(4): 731–744.

Cabantous, L., Gond, J.P., Harding, N. and Learmonth, M. (2016) 'Critical essay: reconsidering critical performativity', *Human Relations*, 69(2): 197–213.

Cahill, D., Primrose, D., Konings, M. and Cooper, M. (2018) 'Introduction: approaches to neoliberalism', in D. Cahill, D. Primrose, M. Konings and M. Cooper (eds) *The SAGE Handbook of Neoliberalism*, London: Sage, pp xxv–xxxiii.

Callahan, J.L. and Elliott, C. (2019) 'Fantasy spaces and emotional derailment: reflections on failure in academic activism', *Organization*, 27(3): 506–514.

Campbell, H., Evans, D. and Murcott, A. (2017) 'Measurability, austerity and edibility: introducing waste into food regime theory', *Journal of Rural Studies*, 51: 168–177.

Caplan, P. (2017) 'Win-win? Food poverty, food aid and food surplus in the UK today', *Anthropology Today*, 33(3): 17–22.

Caraher, M. and Furey, S. (2017) *Is It Appropriate to Use Surplus Food to Feed People in Hunger? Short-Term Band-Aid to More Deep-Rooted Problems of Poverty*, Food Research Collaboration Policy Brief.

Caraher, M. and Furey, S. (2018) *The Economics of Emergency Food Aid Provision*, Cham: Palgrave Pivot.

Chatterton, P. (2006) '"Give up activism" and change the world in unknown ways: or, learning to walk with others on uncommon ground', *Antipode*, 38(2): 259–281.

Chatterton, P. and Pickerill, J. (2010) 'Everyday activism and transitions towards post-capitalist worlds', *Transactions of the Institute of British Geographers*, 35(4): 475–490.

Chatterton, P. and Pusey, A. (2020) 'Beyond capitalist enclosure, commodification and alienation: postcapitalist praxis as commons, social production and useful doing', *Progress in Human Geography*, 44(1): 27–48.

Chatterton, P., Hodkinson, S. and Pickerill, J. (2010) 'Beyond scholar activism: making strategic interventions inside and outside the neoliberal university', *ACME: An International E-Journal for Critical Geographies*, 9(2): 245–275.

Chen, K.K. and Chen, V.T. (2021) '"What if" and "if only" futures beyond conventional capitalism and bureaucracy: imagining collectivist and democratic possibilities for organizing', in K.K. Chen and V.T. Chen (eds) *Organizational Imaginaries: Tempering Capitalism and Tending to Communities through Cooperatives and Collectivist Democracy*, Research in the Sociology of Organizations, Vol 72, Bingley, UK: Emerald Publishing Limited, pp 1–28.

Cheney, G., Santa Cruz, I., Peredo, A.M. and Nazareno, E. (2014) 'Worker cooperatives as an organizational alternative: challenges, achievements and promise in business governance and ownership', *Organization*, 21(5): 591–603.

Chesters, G. (2012) 'Social movements and the ethics of knowledge production', *Social Movement Studies*, 11(2): 145–160.

Choudry, A. (2020) 'Reflections on academia, activism, and the politics of knowledge and learning', *The International Journal of Human Rights*, 24(1): 28–45.

Clapp, J. (2016) *Food* (2nd edn), Cambridge: Polity Press.

Clare, G., Mirosa, M. and Bremer, P. (2023) 'The impact of COVID-19 on food rescue organisations in Aotearoa New Zealand and future crisis management', *British Food Journal*, 125(5): 1895–1913.

Clarke, D. (2022, 10 July) 'Op-ed: want to escape America's Armageddon? Don't come to New Zealand', *Los Angeles Times*, retrieved from: www.latimes.com/opinion/story/2022-07-10/americans-new-zealand-residency-peter-thiel-billionaires-apocaplypse

Clegg, S., Kornberger, M. and Rhodes, C. (2007) 'Organizational ethics, decision making, undecidability', *The Sociological Review*, 55(2): 393–409.

Collins, S. (2014, 20 March) 'Global survey shows one in six Kiwis struggling for food', *New Zealand Herald*, retrieved from: www.nzherald.co.nz/nz/glo bal-survey-shows-one-in-six-kiwis-struggling-for-food/KCJ6CXF73WO V2OPM7FBQLNA5QQ/

Conradson, D. (2008) 'Expressions of charity and action towards justice: faith-based welfare provision in urban New Zealand', *Urban Studies*, 45(10): 2117–2141.

Contu, A. (2018) '"... The point is to change it" – yes, but in what direction and how? Intellectual activism as a way of "walking the talk" of critical work in business schools', *Organization*, 25(2): 282–293.

Contu, A. (2020) 'Answering the crisis with intellectual activism: making a difference as business schools scholars', *Human Relations*, 73(5): 737–757.

Cooke, H. (2017, 12 September) 'Jacinda Ardern says neoliberalism has failed', *Stuff*, retrieved from: www.stuff.co.nz/national/politics/96739673/jacinda-ardern-says-neoliberalism-has-failed

Cox, L. (2015) 'Scholarship and activism: a social movements perspective', *Studies in Social Justice*, 9(1): 34–53.

Crane, A., Soundararajan, V., Bloomfield, M.J., LeBaron, G. and Spence, L.J. (2022) 'Hybrid (un) freedom in worker hostels in garment supply chains', *Human Relations*, 75(10): 1928–1960.

Cunliffe, A.L. (2003) 'Reflexive inquiry in organizational research: questions and possibilities', *Human Relations*, 56(8): 983–1003.

Cunliffe, A.L. (2008) 'Orientations to social constructionism: relationally responsive social constructionism and its implications for knowledge and learning', *Management Learning*, 39(2): 123–139.

Cunliffe, A.L. and Karunanayake, G. (2013) 'Working within hyphen-spaces in ethnographic research: implications for research identities and practice', *Organizational Research Methods*, 16(3): 364–392.

Dahlman, S., Mygind du Plessis, E., Husted, E. and Just, S.N. (2022) 'Alternativity as freedom: exploring tactics of emergence in alternative forms of organizing', *Human Relations*, 75(10): 1961–1985.

Dar, S., Liu, H., Martinez Dy, A. and Brewis, D.N. (2021) 'The business school is racist: act up!', *Organization*, 28(4): 695–706.

Daskalaki, M., Fotaki, M. and Sotiropoulou, I. (2019) 'Performing values practices and grassroots organizing: the case of solidarity economy initiatives in Greece', *Organization Studies*, 40(11): 1741–1765.

DeFilippis, J., Fisher, R. and Shragge, E. (2006) 'Neither romance nor regulation: re-evaluating community', *International Journal of Urban and Regional Research*, 30(3): 673–689.

Del Fa, S. and Vásquez, C. (2019) 'Existing through differentiation: a Derridean approach to alternative organizations', *M@n@gement*, 22(4): 559–583.

Dey, K. and Humphries, M. (2015) 'Recounting food banking: a paradox of counterproductive growth', *Third Sector Review*, 21(2): 129–147.

Diprose, G. and Lee, L. (2022) 'Food rescue as collective care', *Area*, 54(1): 144–151.

Duncanson, M., Oben, G., Wicken, A., Morris, S., McGee, M.A. and Simpson, J. (2017) *Child Poverty Monitor: Technical Report 2017 (National Report)*, Dunedin: New Zealand Child and Youth Epidemiology Service.

Dunne, S., Harney, S. and Parker, M. (2008) 'Speaking out: the responsibilities of management intellectuals: a survey', *Organization*, 15(2): 271–282.

Elmes, M.B. (2018) 'Economic inequality, food insecurity, and the erosion of equality of capabilities in the United States', *Business and Society*, 57(6): 1045–1074.

Ergene, S., Banerjee, S.B. and Hoffman, A.J. (2021) '(Un)sustainability and organization studies: towards a radical engagement', *Organization Studies*, 42(8): 1319–1335.

Escajedo San-Epifanio, L., Inza-Bartolomé, A. and de Renobales Scheifler, M. (2017) 'Food banking', in P.B. Thompson and D.M. Kaplan (eds) *Encyclopedia of Food and Agricultural Ethics*, Dordrecht: Springer, pp 1–7.

Escobar, J.S. (1997) 'Religion and social change at the grass roots in Latin America', *Annals of the American Academy of Political and Social Science*, 554(1): 81–103.

Eskelinen, T. (2020) 'The conception of value in community economies', in T. Eskelinen, T. Hirvilammi and J. Venäläinen (eds) *Enacting Community Economies within a Welfare* State, London: Mayfly, pp 23–45.

Esper, S.C., Cabantous, L., Barin Cruz, L. and Gond, J.P. (2017) 'Supporting alternative organizations? Exploring scholars' involvement in the performativity of worker-recuperated enterprises', *Organization*, 24(5): 671–699.

Evans, D., Campbell, H. and Murcott, A. (2012) 'A brief pre-history of food waste and the social sciences', *The Sociological Review*, 60(S2): 5–26.

Feola, G. (2019) 'Degrowth and the unmaking of capitalism: beyond "decolonization of the imaginary"?', *ACME: An International Journal for Critical Geographies*, 18(4): 977–997.

Fleming, P. (2017) 'The human capital hoax: work, debt and insecurity in the era of Uberization', *Organization Studies*, 38(5): 691–709.

Fleming, P. (2020) 'Dark academia: despair in the neoliberal business school', *Journal of Management Studies*, 57(6): 1305–1311.

Fleming, P. and Banerjee, S.B. (2016) 'When performativity fails: implications for critical management studies', *Human Relations*, 69(2): 257–276.

Food and Agriculture Organization, International Fund for Agricultural Development, UNICEF, World Food Programme and World Health Organization (2023) *The State of Food Security and Nutrition in the World 2023: Urbanization, Agrifood Systems Transformation and Healthy Diets across the Rural–Urban Continuum*, Rome: Food and Agriculture Organization.

Food Banks Canada (2023) *Hunger Count 2023*, Food Banks Canada, retrieved from: https://fbcblobstorage.blob.core.windows.net/wordpress/2023/10/hungercount23-en.pdf

Foucault, M. (1978) *The History of Sexuality. Volume 1: An Introduction*, New York: Random House.

Foucault, M. (1980) *Power/Knowledge: Selected Interviews and Other Writings 1972–1977*, C. Gordon (ed), Brighton: Harvester Wheatsheaf.

Foucault, M. (1982) 'The subject and power', *Critical Inquiry*, 8(4): 777–795.

Foucault, M. (1984) 'On the genealogy of ethics: an overview of work in progress', in P. Rabinow (ed) *The Foucault Reader: An Introduction to Foucault's Thought*, London: Penguin Books, pp 340–372.

Foucault, M. (1991) *Discipline and Punish: The Birth of the Prison*. London: Penguin Books.

Foucault, M. (2008) *The Birth of Biopolitics: Lectures at the Collège de France, 1978–1979*, Basingstoke: Palgrave Macmillan.

Fournier, V. (2013) 'Commoning: on the social organisation of the commons', *M@n@gement*, 16(4): 433–453.

Fraser, N. and Jaeggi, R. (2018) *Capitalism: A Conversation in Critical Theory*, New York: John Wiley & Sons.

Fuller, D. and Jonas, A.E.G. (2003) 'Alternative financial spaces', in A. Leyshon, R. Lee and C.C. Williams (eds) *Alternative Economic Spaces*, London: Sage, pp 55–73.

Fuller, D. and Kitchin, R. (2004) 'Radical theory/critical praxis: academic geography beyond the academy?', in D. Fuller and R. Kitchin (eds) *Radical Theory, Critical Praxis: Making a Difference Beyond the Academy?* ACME e-book series, pp 1–20.

Garthwaite, K. (2016) 'Stigma, shame and "people like us": an ethnographic study of foodbank use in the UK', *Journal of Poverty and Social Justice*, 24(3): 277–289.

Gauthier, F., Martikainen, T. and Woodhead, L. (2013) 'Introduction: religion in market society', in T. Martikainen and F. Gauthier (eds) *Religion in the Neoliberal Age: Political Economy and Modes of Governance*, London: Routledge, pp 1–18.

Gibson-Graham, J.K. (1996) *The End of Capitalism (As We Knew It)*, Minneapolis: University of Minnesota Press.

Gibson-Graham, J.K. (2006) *A Postcapitalist Politics*, Minneapolis: University of Minnesota Press.

Gibson-Graham, J.K. (2008) 'Diverse economies: performative practices for other worlds', *Progress in Human Geography*, 32(5): 613–632.

Gibson-Graham, J.K. (2014) 'Rethinking the economy with thick description and weak theory', *Current Anthropology*, 55(S9): S147–S153.

Gibson-Graham, J.K. (2020) 'Reading for economic difference', in J.K. Gibson-Graham and K. Dombroski (eds) *Handbook of Diverse Economies*, Cheltenham: Edward Elgar, pp 476–485.

Gibson-Graham, J.K. and Dombroski, K. (2020) 'Introduction to the handbook of diverse economies: inventory as ethical intervention', in J.K. Gibson-Graham and K. Dombroski (eds) *Handbook of Diverse Economies*, Cheltenham: Edward Elgar, pp 1–24.

Gibson-Graham, J.K., Cameron, J. and Healy, S. (2013) *Take Back the Economy: An Ethical Guide for Transforming Our Communities*, Minneapolis: University of Minnesota Press.

Gilmore, S., Harding, N., Helin, J. and Pullen, A. (2019) 'Writing differently', *Management Learning*, 50(1): 3–10.

Giroux, H.A. (2014) *Neoliberalism's War on Higher Education*, Chicago: Haymarket Books.

Gómez Garrido, M., Carbonero Gamundí, M.A. and Viladrich, A. (2019) 'The role of grassroots food banks in building political solidarity with vulnerable people', *European Societies*, 21(5): 753–773.

Goodman-Smith, F., Mirosa, M. and Skeaff, S. (2020) 'A mixed-methods study of retail food waste in New Zealand', *Food Policy*, 92: 101845. doi: 10.1016/j.foodpol.2020.101845

Graeber, D. (2001) *Toward an Anthropological Theory of Value: The False Coin of Our Own Dreams*, New York: Palgrave Macmillan.

Grosser, K. (2021) 'Gender, business and human rights: academic activism as critical engagement in neoliberal times', *Gender, Work & Organization*, 28(4): 1624–1637.

Growing Up in New Zealand (2023, 1 May) 'Now we are 12. Snapshot 3: food insecurity', *Growing Up in New Zealand*, retrieved from: www.growingup.co.nz/growing-up-report/food-insecurity

Gümüsay, A.A. (2020) 'The potential for plurality and prevalence of the religious institutional logic', *Business & Society*, 59(5): 855–880.

Gümüsay, A.A. and Reinecke, J. (2022) 'Researching for desirable futures: from real utopias to imagining alternatives', *Journal of Management Studies*, 59(1): 236–242.

Gustafsson, U., O'Connell, R., Draper, A. and Tonner, A. (2019) *What is Food?* Abingdon: Routledge.

Hardt, M. and Negri, A. (2017) *Assembly*, Oxford: Oxford University Press.

Hardt, M. and Negri, A. (2001) *Empire*, Cambridge, MA: Harvard University Press.

Harvey, D. (2007) *A Brief History of Neoliberalism*, Oxford: Oxford University Press.

Harvey, D. (2010) *The Enigma of the Capital and the Crises of Capitalism*, Oxford: Oxford University Press.

Harvey, D. (2014) *Seventeen Contradictions and the End of Capitalism*, London: Profile Books.

Harvie, D. and Milburn, K. (2010) 'How organizations value and how value organizes', *Organization*, 17(5): 631–636.

Healy, S. (2009) 'Economies, alternative', in R. Kitchin and N. Thrift (eds) *International Encyclopedia of Human Geography*, Vol 3, Oxford: Elsevier, pp 338–344.

Healy, S., Selcuk, C. and Madra, Y. (2020) 'Framing essay: subjectivity in a diverse economy', in J.K. Gibson-Graham and K. Dombroski (eds) *Handbook of Diverse Economies*, Cheltenham: Edward Elgar, pp 389–401.

History of the SMRSC Conference (2020) 'Social Movements, Resistance and Social Change conference', retrieved from: www.socialmovementsaotearoa.com/

Holloway, J. (2002) 'Twelve theses on changing the world without taking power', *The Commoner*, 4: 1–6.

Holt-Giménez, E. (2019) 'Capitalism, food, and social movements: the political economy of food system transformation', *Journal of Agriculture, Food Systems, and Community Development*, 9(1): 1–13.

Howard, P.H. (2016) *Concentration and Power in the Food System: Who Controls What We Eat?* London: Bloomsbury.

Huang, C.H., Liu, S.M. and Hsu, N.Y. (2020) 'Understanding global food surplus and food waste to tackle economic and environmental sustainability', *Sustainability*, 12(7): 2892. doi: 10.3390/su12072892

Humpage, L. (2014) *Policy Change, Public Attitudes and Social Citizenship: Does Neoliberalism Matter?* Bristol: Policy Press.

Humphrey, C. and Hugh-Jones, S. (eds) (1992) *Barter, Exchange and Value: An Anthropological Approach*, Cambridge: Cambridge University Press.

Invest New Zealand (2023) 'Food and beverage', *Invest New Zealand*, retrieved from: www.nzte.govt.nz/page/food-and-beverage

Janssens, M. and Zanoni, P. (2021) 'Making diversity research matter for social change: new conversations beyond the firm', *Organization Theory*, 2(2): 1–21.

Jaques, N., Jones, C., Murtola, A.M. and Walsh, S. (2016) 'Radical returns', *New Zealand Sociology*, 31(6): 1–9.

Jensen, M.C. (2002) 'Value maximization, stakeholder theory, and the corporate objective function', *Business Ethics Quarterly*, 12(2): 235–256.

Jessop, B. (2018) 'Neoliberalism and workfare: Schumpeterian or Ricardian?', in D. Cahill, D. Primrose, M. Konings and M. Cooper (eds) *The SAGE Handbook of Neoliberalism*, London: Sage, pp 347–358.

Johnson, A. (2018) *Kei a Tātou: It Is Us. State of the Nation Report*, Auckland: The Salvation Army Social Policy and Parliamentary Unit, retrieved from: www.salvationarmy.org.nz/KeiaTatou

Jonas, A.E.G. (2013) 'Interrogating alternative local and regional economies: the British credit union movement and post-binary thinking', in H.-M. Zademach and S. Hillebrand (eds) *Alternative Economies and Spaces: New Perspectives for a Sustainable Economy*, Bielefeld: Transcript, pp 23–42.

Jones, D.R., Visser, M., Stokes, P., Örtenblad, A., Deem, R., Rodgers, P. and Tarba, S.Y. (2020) 'The performative university: "targets", "terror" and "taking back freedom" in academia', *Management Learning*, 51(4): 363–377.

Just, S.N., De Cock, C. and Schaefer, S.M. (2021) 'From antagonists to allies? Exploring the critical performativity of alternative organization', *Culture and Organization*, 27(2): 89–97.

Kaplan, D.M. (2019) *Food Philosophy: An Introduction*, New York: Columbia University Press.

Kavanagh, D. (2009) 'Institutional heterogeneity and change: the university as fool', *Organization*, 16(4): 575–595.

Kelsey, J. (1995) *The New Zealand Experiment*, Auckland: Bridget Williams Books.

King, D. (2015) 'The possibilities and perils of critical performativity: learning from four case studies', *Scandinavian Journal of Management*, 31(2): 255–265.

King, D. and Land, C. (2018) 'The democratic rejection of democracy: performative failure and the limits of critical performativity in an organizational change project', *Human Relations*, 71(11): 1535–1557.

Klein, J.A. and Watson, J.L. (eds) (2016) *The Handbook of Food and Anthropology*, London: Bloomsbury Academic.

Kneafsey, M., Maye, D., Holloway, L. and Goodman, M.K. (2021) *Geographies of Food: An Introduction*, London: Bloomsbury Academic.

Knights, D. (2002) 'Writing organizational analysis into Foucault', *Organization*, 9(4), 575–593.

Koç, M., Sumner, J. and Winson, A. (2016) *Critical Perspectives in Food Studies* (2nd edn), Oxford: Oxford University Press.

Kociatkiewicz, J., Kostera, M. and Parker, M. (2021) 'The possibility of disalienated work: being at home in alternative organizations', *Human Relations*, 74(7): 933–957.

Kokkinidis, G. (2015) 'Spaces of possibilities: workers' self-management in Greece', *Organization*, 22(6): 847–871.

Kokkinidis, G. and Checchi, M. (2023) 'Power matters: posthuman entanglements in a social solidarity clinic', *Organization*, 30(2): 288–306.

Lacan, J. (2007) *The Seminar of Jacques Lacan: The Other Side of Psychoanalysis (Book XVII)*, New York: WW Norton & Company.

Lambie-Mumford, H. and Dowler, E. (2014) 'Rising use of "food aid" in the United Kingdom', *British Food Journal*, 116(9): 1418–1425.

Lepak, D.P., Smith, K.G. and Taylor, M.S. (2007) 'Value creation and value capture: a multilevel perspective', *Academy of Management Review*, 32(1): 180–194.

Levkoe, C. and Wakefield, S. (2011) 'The Community Food Centre: creating space for a just, sustainable, and healthy food system', *Journal of Agriculture, Food Systems, and Community Development*, 2(1): 249–268.

Levy, D., Reinecke, J. and Manning, S. (2016) 'The political dynamics of sustainable coffee: contested value regimes and the transformation of sustainability', *Journal of Management Studies*, 53(3): 364–401.

Lindebaum, D., den Hond, F., Greenwood, M., Chamberlain, J.A. and Andersson, L. (2022) 'Freedom, work and organizations in the 21st century: freedom for whom and for whose purpose?', *Human Relations*, 75(10): 1853–1874.

Lindenbaum, J. (2015) 'Countermovement, neoliberal platoon, or re-gifting depot? Understanding decommodification in US food banks', *Antipode*, 48(2): 375–392.

MacCallum, G.C.J. (2006) 'Negative and positive freedom', in D. Miller (ed) *The Liberty Reader*, Abingdon: Routledge, pp 100–122.

Macfarlane, B. (2021) 'The conceit of activism in the illiberal university', *Policy Futures in Education*, 19(5): 594–606.

Mainvil, L., Mirosa, M., Chisnall, S.J., Jones, E., Marshall, J. and Wassilak, C. (2018) *Food Waste in the Cafe & Restaurant Sector in New Zealand*, Wasteminz, retrieved from: https://ourarchive.otago.ac.nz/bitstream/handle/10523/12171/New-Zealand-cafe-and-resturant-food-waste-WasteMINZ-2018.pdf?sequence=1&isAllowed=y

Malinowski, B. (2002) *Argonauts of the Western Pacific: An Account of Native Enterprise and Adventure in the Archipelagoes of Melanesian New Guinea*, London: Routledge.

Marcus, G.E. (1995) 'Ethnography in/of the world system: the emergence of multi-sited ethnography', *Annual Review of Anthropology*, 24: 95–117.

Marx, K. (1844) 'A contribution to the critique of Hegel's philosophy of right', *Marxists Internet Archive*, retrieved from: www.marxists.org/archive/marx/works/1843/critique-hpr/intro.htm

Marx, K. (1990) *Capital: A Critique of Political Economy*, Vol 1 (Trans B. Fowkes), New York: Penguin.

Mauss, M. (1990) *The Gift: The Form and Reason for Exchange in Archaic Societies*, Abingdon: Routledge.

Maxey, I. (1999) 'Beyond boundaries? Activism, academia, reflexivity and research', *Area*, 31(3): 199–208.

McKinnon, K. (2020) 'Framing essay: the diversity of labour', in J.K. Gibson-Graham and K. Dombroski (eds) *Handbook of Diverse Economies*, Cheltenham, UK: Edward Elgar, pp 116–128.

Mika, J.P., Fahey, N. and Bensemann, J. (2019) 'What counts as an indigenous enterprise? Evidence from Aotearoa New Zealand', *Journal of Enterprising Communities: People and Places in the Global Economy*, 13(3): 372–390.

Miller, J. and Deutsch, J. (2009) *Food Studies: An Introduction to Research Methods*, Oxford: Berg.

Ministry of Business, Innovation and Employment (2022) 'Growing the food and beverage sector', *Ministry of Business, Innovation and Employment*, retrieved from: www.mbie.govt.nz/business-and-employment/economic-development/growing-the-food-and-beverage-sector/

Mirosa, M., Mainvil, L., Horne, H. and Mangan-Walker, E. (2016) 'The social value of rescuing food, nourishing communities', *British Food Journal*, 118(12): 3044–3058.

Möller, C. (2021) 'Discipline and feed: food banks, pastoral power, and the medicalisation of poverty in the UK', *Sociological Research Online*, 26(4): 853–870.

Mondon-Navazo, M., Murgia, A., Borghi, P. and Mezihorak, P. (2022) 'In search of alternatives for individualised workers: A comparative study of freelance organisations', *Organization*, 29(4): 736–756.

Monticelli, L. (2021) 'On the necessity of prefigurative politics', *Thesis Eleven*, 167(1): 99–118.

Moser, C., Reinecke, J., den Hond, F., Svejenova, S. and Croidieu, G. (2021) 'Biomateriality and organizing: towards an organizational perspective on food', *Organization Studies*, 42(2): 175–193.

Murcott, A. (2013) 'A burgeoning field: introduction to the Handbook of Food Research', in A. Murcott, W. Belasco and P. Jackson (eds) *The Handbook of Food Research*, London: Bloomsbury, pp 1–25.

Murcott, A. (2019) *Introducing the Sociology of Food and Eating*, London: Bloomsbury Publishing.

Murcott, A., Belasco, W. and Jackson, P. (eds) (2013) *The Handbook of Food Research*, London: Bloomsbury.

Mylek, I. and Nel, P. (2010) 'Religion and relief: the role of religion in mobilizing civil society against global poverty', *Kōtuitui: New Zealand Journal of Social Sciences Online*, 5(2): 81–97.

Nazir, O. (2021) *Critical Insights into Modern Slavery: Case of Debt Bonded Labour in Indian Brick Kilns*, Unpublished PhD thesis, Massey University, New Zealand.

Newton, T. (1998) 'Theorizing subjectivity in organizations: the failure of Foucauldian studies?', *Organization Studies*, 19(3): 415–447.

Nørgård, R.T. and Bengtsen, S.S. (2021) 'The activist university and university activism – an editorial', *Policy Futures in Education*, 19(5): 507–512.

New Zealand Food Network (2023a) *Side By Side: Improving Food Security*, Auckland: New Zealand Food Network, retrieved from: www.nzfoodnetwork.org.nz/our-impact/

New Zealand Food Network (2023b) 'Side by side: summer 2023', *New Zealand Food Network*, retrieved from: https://go.nzfoodnetwork.org.nz/webmail/878952/495985326/fdb435cb2d9a77619ee1b374d9e6bfe5b96904d6b9ceb4c12bbdfe5fdf63997a

O'Brien, M. (2012) 'A "lasting transformation" of capitalist surplus: from food stocks to feedstocks', *The Sociological Review*, 60(2): 192–211.

Oxford English Dictionary (nd) 'Dispositive', *Oxford English Dictionary*, retrieved from: www.oed.com/view/Entry/55126?redirectedFrom=disp ositive#eid

Pansera, M. and Rizzi, F. (2020) 'Furbish or perish: Italian social cooperatives at a crossroads', *Organization*, 27(1): 17–35.

Parker, M. (2018) *Shut Down the Business School*, London: Pluto Press.

Parker, M. (2021) 'The critical business school and the university: a case study of resistance and co-optation', *Critical Sociology*, 47(7–8): 1111–1124.

Parker, M. (2023) 'The university without walls: space, time and capacities', *Learning and Teaching*, 16(2): 13–31.

Parker, M. and Thomas, R. (2011) 'What is a critical journal?', *Organization*, 18(4): 419–427.

Parker, M., Cheney, G., Fournier, V. and Land, C. (2014a) 'The question of organization: a manifesto for alternatives', *ephemera*, 14(4): 623–638.

Parker, M., Cheney, G., Fournier, V. and Land, C. (eds) (2014b) *The Routledge Companion to Alternative Organization*, London: Routledge.

Parker, S. and Parker, M. (2017) 'Antagonism, accommodation and agonism in critical management studies: alternative organisations as allies', *Human Relations*, 70(11): 1366–1387.

Peck, J. (2018) 'Preface: naming neoliberalism', in D. Cahill, D. Primrose, M. Konings and M. Cooper (eds) *The SAGE Handbook of Neoliberalism*, London: Sage, pp xxii–xxiv.

Peck, J. and Tickell, A. (2002) 'Neoliberalizing space', *Antipode*, 34(3): 380–404.

Peltonen, T. (2017) *Spirituality and Religion In Organizing: Beyond Secular Leadership*, Cham: Springer.

Peredo, A.M. and Chrisman, J.J. (2006) 'Toward a theory of community-based enterprise', *Academy of Management Review*, 31(2): 309–328.

Peredo, A.M. and McLean, M. (2020) 'Decommodification in action: common property as countermovement', *Organization*, 27(6): 817–839.

Pilcher, J.M. (ed) (2012) *The Oxford Handbook of Food History*, Oxford: Oxford University Press.

Pina e Cunha, M., Cabral-Cardoso, C. and Clegg, S. (2008) 'Manna from heaven: the exuberance of food as a topic for research in management and organization', *Human Relations*, 61(7): 935–963.

Pitelis, C.N. (2009) 'The co-evolution of organizational value capture, value creation and sustainable advantage', *Organization Studies*, 30(10): 1115–1139.

Pitts, H. (2021) *Value*, Cambridge: Polity.

Pitzer, D.E., Janzen, D.E., Lewis, D. and Wright-Summerton, R. (2014) 'Communes and intentional communities', in M. Parker, G. Cheney, V. Fournier and C. Land (eds) *The Routledge Companion to Alternative Organization*, London: Routledge, pp 89–104.

Polanyi, K. (2001) *The Great Transformation: The Political and Economic Origins of Our Time* (2nd edn), Boston: Beacon Press.

Poppendieck, J. (1998) *Sweet Charity*, London: Penguin.

Power, M., Small, N., Doherty, B., Stewart-Knox, B. and Pickett, K.E. (2017) '"Bringing heaven down to earth": the purpose and place of religion in UK food aid', *Social Enterprise Journal*, 13(3): 251–267.

Prichard, C. (2015) 'Seven steps to excellentristic research', *Academy of Management Proceedings*, 2015(1). doi: 10.5465/ambpp.2015.11678abstract

Prichard, C. (2016) 'Value: an inquiry into relations, forms and struggles', in R. Mir, H. Willmott and M. Greenwood (eds) *The Routledge Companion to Philosophy in Organization Studies*, Abingdon: Routledge, pp 575–583.

Prichard, C. and Mir, R. (2010) 'Editorial: organizing value', *Organization*, 17(5): 507–515.

Prichard, C. and Benschop, Y. (2018) 'It's time for acting up!', *Organization*, 25(1): 98–105.

Prichard, C. and Alakavuklar, O.N. (2019) 'Changing the critique: from critical management studies to activist scholarship', in A. Sturdy, S. Heusinkveld, T. Reay and D. Strang (eds) *The Oxford Handbook of Management Ideas*, Oxford: Oxford University Press, pp 473–491.

Prokou, E. (2008) 'The emphasis on employability and the changing role of the university in Europe', *Higher Education in Europe*, 33(4): 387–394.

Pullen, A. (2018) 'Writing as labiaplasty', *Organization*, 25(1): 123–130.

Pullen, A. and Rhodes, C. (2018) 'Anxiety and organisation', *Culture and Organization*, 24(2): 95–99.

Rabinow, P. and Rose, N. (2003) 'Foucault today', in P. Rabinow and N. Rose (eds) *The Essential Foucault: Selections from the Essential Works of Foucault, 1954–1984*, New York: New Press, pp vii–xxxv.

Radio New Zealand (2023, 23 May) '"Hundreds of thousands" of Kiwis don't have money for food as demand at foodbanks increase', *Radio New Zealand*, retrieved from: www.rnz.co.nz/news/national/490464/hundreds-of-thousands-of-kiwis-don-t-have-money-for-food-as-demand-at-foodbanks-increase

Raffnsøe, S., Gudmand-Høyer, M. and Thaning, M.S. (2016) 'Foucault's dispositive: the perspicacity of dispositive analytics in organizational research', *Organization*, 23(2): 272–298.

Raffnsøe, S., Mennicken, A. and Miller, P. (2019) 'The Foucault effect in organization studies', *Organization Studies*, 40(2): 155–182.

Rashbrooke, M. (ed) (2013) *Inequality: A New Zealand Crisis*, Wellington: Bridget Williams Books.

Ratle, O., Robinson, S., Bristow, A. and Kerr, R. (2020) 'Mechanisms of micro-terror? Early career CMS academics' experiences of "targets and terror" in contemporary business schools', *Management Learning*, 51(4): 452–471.

Redden, G., Phelan, S. and Baker, C. (2020) 'Different routes up the same mountain? Neoliberalism in Australia and New Zealand', in S. Dawes and M. Lenormand (eds) *Neoliberalism in Context: Governance, Subjectivity and Knowledge*, Cham: Palgrave Macmillan, pp 61–82.

Reed, M. (2006) 'Organizational theorizing: a historically contested terrain', in S. Clegg, C. Hardy, T. Lawrence and W.R. Nord (eds) *The SAGE Handbook of Organization Studies*, London: Sage, pp 19–54.

Reedy, P. and Learmonth, M. (2009) 'Other possibilities? The contribution to management education of alternative organisations', *Management Learning*, 40(3): 241–258.

Reedy, P. and King, D. (2019) 'Critical performativity in the field: methodological principles for activist ethnographers', *Organizational Research Methods*, 22(2): 564–589.

Reedy, P., King, D. and Coupland, C. (2016) 'Organizing for individuation: alternative organizing, politics and new identities', *Organization Studies*, 37(11): 1553–1573.

Rehn, A. (2014) 'Gifts, gifting and gift economies: on challenging capitalism with blood, plunder and necklaces', in M. Parker, G. Cheney, V. Fournier and C. Land (eds) *The Routledge Companion to Alternative Organization*, London: Routledge, pp 195–209.

Reiter, B. and Oslender, U. (2015) *Bridging Scholarship and Activism: Reflections from the Frontlines of Collaborative Research*, East Lansing: Michigan State University Press.

Resnick, S. and Wolff, R. (2013) 'On overdetermination and Althusser: our response to Silverman and Park', *Rethinking Marxism*, 25(3): 341–349.

Reynolds, C.J., Mirosa, M. and Clothier, B. (2016) 'New Zealand's food waste: estimating the tonnes, value, calories and resources wasted', *Agriculture*, 6(1): 9. doi: 10.3390/agriculture6010009

Reynolds, D., Mirosa, M. and Campbell, H. (2020) 'Food and vulnerability in Aotearoa/New Zealand: a review and theoretical reframing of food insecurity, income and neoliberalism', *New Zealand Sociology*, 35(1): 123–152.

Rhodes, C., Wright, C. and Pullen, A. (2018) 'Changing the world? The politics of activism and impact in the neoliberal university', *Organization*, 25(1): 139–147.

Riches, G. (2011) 'Thinking and acting outside the charitable food box: hunger and the right to food in rich societies', *Development in Practice*, 21(4–5): 768–775.

Riches, G. (2018) *Food Bank Nations: Poverty, Corporate Charity and the Right to Food*, Abingdon: Routledge.

Rose, N. (2001) 'The politics of life itself', *Theory, Culture and Society*, 18(6): 1–30.

Ruth, D., Wilson, S., Alakavuklar, O.N. and Dickson, A. (2018) 'Anxious academics: talking back to the audit culture through collegial, critical and creative autoethnography', *Culture and Organization*, 24(2): 154–170.

Sage, C. (ed) (2022) *A Research Agenda for Food Systems*, Cheltenham: Edward Elgar.

Salonen, A.S. (2016) 'Locating religion in the context of charitable food assistance: an ethnographic study of food banks in a Finnish city', *Journal of Contemporary Religion*, 31(1): 35–50.

Salonen, A. (2018) 'Religion, poverty, and abundance', *Palgrave Communications*, 4: 27.

Schad, J., Lewis, M.W., Raisch, S. and Smith, W.K. (2016) 'Paradox research in management science: looking back to move forward', *Academy of Management Annals*, 10(1): 5–64.

Schiller-Merkens, S. (2022) 'Prefiguring an alternative economy: understanding prefigurative organizing and its struggles', *Organization*. doi: 10.1177/13505084221124189

Schmid, B. (2021) 'Alternative/diverse economies', in D. Richardson, N. Castree, M.F. Goodchild, A. Kobayashi, W. Liu and R.A. Marston (eds) *International Encyclopedia of Geography*, Wiley. doi: 10.1002/9781118786352. wbieg2125

Schrag, Z.M. (2011) 'The case against ethics review in the social sciences', *Research Ethics*, 7(4): 120–131.

Seyfang, G. and Smith, A. (2007) 'Grassroots innovations for sustainable development: towards a new research and policy agenda', *Environmental Politics*, 16(4): 584–603.

Shukaitis, S. and Graeber, D. (2007) 'Introduction', in S. Shukaitis, D. Graeber and E. Biddle (eds) *Constituent Imagination: Militant Investigations/Collective Theorisation*. Oakland, CA: AK Press, pp 11–34.

Springer, S., Birch, K. and MacLeavy, J. (2016) 'An introduction to neoliberalism', in S. Springer, K. Birch and J. MacLeavy (eds) *The Handbook of Neoliberalism*, London: Routledge, pp 1–14.

Stats NZ (2019, 3 October) 'Losing our religion', *Stats NZ*, retrieved from: www.stats.govt.nz/news/losing-our-religion

Strong, S. (2020) 'Food banks, actually existing austerity and the localisation of responsibility', *Geoforum*, 110: 211–219.

Stuart, T. (2009) *Waste: Uncovering the Global Food Scandal*, London: Penguin.

Sutherland, N. (2012) 'Book review: Social movements and activist ethnography', *Organization*, 20(4): 627–635.

Sutherland, N., Land, C. and Böhm, S. (2014) 'Anti-leaders (hip) in social movement organizations: the case of autonomous grassroots groups', *Organization*, 21(6): 759–781.

Szende, J. (2015) 'Food deserts, justice and the distributive paradigm', in J.M. Dieterle (ed) *Just Food: Philosophy, Justice and Food*, London: Rowman and Littlefield, pp 57–67.

Tanielu, R.O.N.J.I. (2021) *Food for Thought: Disrupting Food Insecurity in Aotearoa*, Auckland: The Salvation Army Social Policy and Parliamentary Unit.

Tarasuk, V. and Eakin, J.M. (2005) 'Food assistance through "surplus" food: insights from an ethnographic study of food bank work', *Agriculture and Human Values*, 22(2): 177–186.

Taylor, D. (2016) 'A resurgent left', *Counterfutures*, 2: 9–20.

Taylor, D. (2017) 'Activism and academia', *Global Dialogue*, 7(3): 28–29.

Tedmanson, D., Essers, C., Dey, P. and Verduyn, K. (2015) 'An *uncommon* wealth ... transforming the commons with purpose, for people and not for profit!', *Journal of Management Inquiry*, 24(4): 439–444.

The Trussell Trust (2023, 16 April) 'Record number of emergency food parcels provided to people facing hardship by Trussell Trust food banks in past 12 months', *The Trussell Trust*, retrieved from: www.trusselltrust.org/2023/04/26/record-number-of-emergency-food-parcels-provided-to-people-facing-hardship-by-trussell-trust-food-banks-in-past-12-months/

Thomas, G. (2015) *How to Do Your Case Study*, London: Sage.

Timmermans, S. and Tavory, I. (2012) 'Theory construction in qualitative research: from grounded theory to abductive analysis', *Sociological Theory*, 30(3): 167–186.

Tourish, D. (2020) 'The triumph of nonsense in management studies', *Academy of Management Learning and Education*, 19(1): 99–109.

Tracey, P., Phillips, N. and Lounsbury, M. (2014) 'Taking religion seriously in the study of organizations', *Religion and Organization Theory*, 41: 3–21.

United Nations Development Programme (nd) 'New Zealand', *United Nations Development Programme*, retrieved from: https://hdr.undp.org/data-center/specific-country-data#/countries/NZL

United Nations Environment Programme (2021) *Food Waste Index Report 2021*, Nairobi: United Nations Environment Programme.

Utting, P. (2015) 'Introduction: the challenge of scaling up social and solidarity economy', in P. Utting (ed) *Social and Solidarity Economy: Beyond the Fringe?*, London: Zed Books, pp 1–37.

Van Buren, H.J., Syed, J. and Mir, R. (2020) 'Religion as a macro social force affecting business: concepts, questions, and future research', *Business and Society*, 59(5): 799–822.

van Dyk, S. (2018) 'Post-wage politics and the rise of community capitalism', *Work, Employment and Society*, 32(3): 528–545.

Van Maanen, J., Sørensen, J.B. and Mitchell, T.R. (2007) 'The interplay between theory and method', *Academy of Management Review*, 32(4): 1145–1154.

Vidaillet, B. and Bousalham, Y. (2020) 'Coworking spaces as places where economic diversity can be articulated: towards a theory of syntopia', *Organization*, 27(1): 60–87.

Villadsen, K. (2021) '"The dispositive": Foucault's concept for organizational analysis?', *Organization Studies*, 42(3): 473–494.

Villadsen, K. (2023) 'Goodbye Foucault's "missing human agent"? Self-formation, capability and the dispositifs', *European Journal of Social Theory*, 26(1): 67–89.

Vlaholias, E., Thompson, K., Every, D. and Dawson, D. (2015) 'Charity starts … at work? Conceptual foundations for research with businesses that donate to food redistribution organisations', *Sustainability*, 7(6): 7997–8021.

Warshawsky, D.N. (2016) 'Food waste, sustainability, and the corporate sector: case study of a US food company', *The Geographical Journal*, 182(4): 384–394.

Watson, D.J. (2020) 'Working the fields: the organization of labour in community supported agriculture', *Organization*, 27(2): 291–313.

Watson, F. and Ekici, A. (2020) 'Understanding the dark sides of alternative economies to maximize societal benefit', *Journal of Macromarketing*, 40(2): 169–184.

Watson, S. (2019) 'Food banks and food rescue organisations: damned if they do; damned if they don't', *Aotearoa New Zealand Social Work*, 31(4): 72–83.

Weatherall, R. (2021) *Reimagining Academic Activism: Learning from Feminist Anti-Violence Activists*, Bristol: Policy Press.

Weiskopf, R. and Loacker, B. (2006) '"A snake's coils are even more intricate than a mole's burrow": individualisation and subjectification in post-disciplinary regimes of work', *Management Revue*, 17(4): 395–419.

Wharerata Writing Group (2018) 'Critical management studies', in C. Cassell, A. Cunliffe and G. Grandy (eds) *The Sage Handbook of Qualitative Research Methods in Business and Management*, London: Sage, pp 69–85.

White, R.J. and Williams, C.C. (2016) 'Beyond capitalocentricism: are non-capitalist work practices "alternatives"?', *Area*, 48(3): 325–331.

Willatt, A. (2018) 'Re-envisaging research on "alternatives" through participatory inquiry: co-generating knowledge on the social practice of care in a community kitchen', *ephemera*, 18(4): 767–790.

Williams, A., Cloke, P. and Thomas, S. (2012) 'Co-constituting neoliberalism: faith-based organisations, co-option, and resistance in the UK', *Environment and Planning A*, 44(6): 1479–1501.

Woolf, A.L. (2020, 13 February) 'The world's "tragically high" food waste problem is worse than previously thought', *Stuff*, retrieved from: www.stuff.co.nz/environment/climate-news/119449508/the-worlds-tragically-high-food-waste-problem-is-worse-than-previously-thought

World Bank (nd) 'GDP per capita (current US$) – New Zealand', *World Bank*, retrieved from: https://data.worldbank.org/indicator/NY.GDP.PCAP.CD?locations=NZ

World Food Programme (2023, 23 October) 'WFP at a glance', *World Food Programme*, retrieved from: www.wfp.org/stories/wfp-glance

Wright, E.O. (2012) 'Transforming capitalism through real utopias', *American Sociological Review*, 78(1): 1–25.

Wright, E.O. (2019) *How to Be an Anticapitalist in the Twenty-First Century*, London: Verso Books.

Ybema, S., Yanow, D., Wels, H. and Kamsteeg, F.H. (2009) 'Studying everyday organizational life', in S. Ybema, D. Yanow, H. Wels and F.H. Kamsteeg (eds) *Organizational Ethnography: Studying the Complexity of Everyday Life*, London: Sage, pp 1–20.

Zanoni, P. (2020) 'Prefiguring alternatives through the articulation of post- and anti-capitalistic politics: an introduction to three additional papers and a reflection', *Organization*, 27(1): 3–16.

Zanoni, P., Contu, A., Healy, S. and Mir, R. (2017) 'Post-capitalistic politics in the making: the imaginary and praxis of alternative economies', *Organization*, 24(5): 575–588.

Index

References to figures appear in *italic* type; those in **bold** type refer to tables.